Between the Bars:
A New Framework for Creating Change in Social Justice

Leah R Kyaio

DEDICATION

As is the way of my tradition, I dedicate this book to the Seventh Generation, to the healing and empowering forward and backward, standing on the shoulders of my Ancestors.

Contents

ACKNOWLEDGMENTS

Nothing is ever accomplished alone. I am never alone. There are many who have made this work possible.

Each of you who grow and learn with me in trainings, coaching, and so much more, thank you.

To Rose Blackfeather (Momma), Mattie, Patty, and Michah whose short lives impacted me to be who I am in this work. I speak your names.

To Ebie, my ever-present cheerleader, partner in mischief and business, and with whom I walk this journey.

To Jules, whose encouragement and constant reminder that this work needed to be out in the world and, most importantly, with the push to write from the heart really made this happen in a good way.

To those who helped to edit, served as sound boards, and supported me in the doing of the things; you know who you are.

Miigwech.

Introduction

What if much of what's done in the name of diversity is all wrong?

Not such far a stretch considering we've been doing the work for over 50 years with little to no change. We see lines being drawn based on skin color, political parties, support of one group in exclusion of another (ie you can support either Black Lives Matter or law enforcement), even divisions within religious organizations that have historically banded together.

What's gone wrong?

One of the problems is that the current model of diversity, equity, and inclusion (DEI) starts in the middle of the conversation. It tends to point fingers at people and tell them they have to have these conversations, look at these perspectives, believe this or that, make this change in policy or practice, and (often) if they don't or can't, there's something terribly wrong with them and their moral compass.

The biggest disconnection is that few have the skills, tools, and strategies to actually engage in those conversations effectively, to be able explore their beliefs, or consider other perspectives, let alone create best practices and policies. Because of that disconnection, the information feels like a challenge and the response is defensiveness that often quickly deteriorates to name calling or, worse, divisiveness.

We need to stop telling people what they need to believe, how they have to think, or in other ways stand in judgement and condemnation. That's the shame and blame model that hasn't served us well. That's the model where, when diversity content is delivered through it, we actually create divisiveness and hostility – in individuals, organizations, and society. It creates us versus them. It's trying to teach inclusion by modeling exclusion. It doesn't work.

What happens if, instead, as the result of common framework and common language, we have the opportunity to learn and practice the tools and skills to engage in the difficult dialogue, to remain respectful and drive to mutual, productive change, even if we don't agree, don't share the same experience, or think the same way?

In my experience, this is what leads to changes in behavior, the result of clearer understanding of what oppression is, how and who it impacts, and our role in making change. Those changes of behavior are changes to respectful behavior and language in professional (and personal) interactions. That's the path that takes us forward.

To be clear, this is about the work of moving the process forward, of creating positive change in areas of social justice. We will never eliminate racism, sexism, heterosexism, etc. But lots of people do or say harmful things because they don't understand what's happening internally or externally. They've never been given a framework that they can wrap their head around, that can help them go deep, understand things they don't experience.

Instead, they are chastised, "called out," and/or shut down. They often then find themselves on the sidelines. They become silent even though the rhetoric tells them silence is complicit. They don't know what to do, what skills and tools they need, or where to get them. How will they learn if we don't bring them to the table to begin the conversation, really diving into the content?

After more than 25 years in the field of diversity I offer the Cage of Oppression and the lens it affords as a new framework that allows us to know, comprehend, apply, analyze, synthesize, and evaluate content we have come to know as DEI, social justice, equity justice, etc. This is how we wrap our brains around a complex reality in a concrete way that we can manipulate and extrapolate to allow us to go deeper and deeper into the needed conversations. *It doesn't make those conversations easier or more comfortable*. It does, however, make them more possible and accessible.

Again, we will not eliminate white supremacy, colonization, or oppression in my lifetime. But we have to start and continue doing the work. We need to start with what we *can* do; begin to increase the number of people who can recognize it, call it forward, talk about it, and begin to make the changes in their own behavior while supporting that change in those around them and the organizations they serve. Most importantly, we are using tools and strategies that allow clear boundaries to ensure our personal and collective safety while we explore the challenging content. THAT is the work we need to be doing right now. That's what this book is all about.

Between the Bars lays out the foundations of how we can begin to change the conversations, how we can have the common framework of the Cage of Oppression that provides the common language to engage in meaningful, difficult, uncomfortable conversations that move us forward. It's where we learn and practice new tools and skills of communication, conflict negotiation, and self-management. It is how we can truly embrace rich diversity – even and especially when we don't agree - and still be respectful and productive. It's the beginning of learning, exploring, and practicing the tools, strategies, and skills to move this work forward, making positive change for everyone.

Sounds like a lot in such a small book, eh? I've been doing this a long time with great success. I promise we will lay all of the foundations by the time we finish. Additionally, the eBook series, Deep Dive, (the "sequels") will take these conversations even deeper.

Can't wait to share it all with you!

The Beginnings

Every culture has a variation of a "creation" story. That creation story is packed with meaning on levels beyond just the ideas of how the world, or in this case framework, came to be. It illustrates how things relate to one another and what other treasures there are within the cultural ideals and concepts. This is true for this work as we explore the forming of the bars and the developing of the framework in what I know as The Cage of Oppression.

The origins of the Cage framework are clear. It is the journey throughout my work that has added, adapted, and made the work meaningful and the opportunities for tools and concept development rich and exciting. The goal is you (collective "you" and individual "you") can use it as a leaping point to go even further. But I'm getting ahead of myself.

The metaphor of oppression as a birdcage was originally coined by Marilyn Frye in the 1970s[1]. The general idea is that, if there was a single bar that was necessary to negotiate, it would be easy to just go around it. But oppression, systemically, doesn't function that way. There are bars all around us and consequently, the navigation becomes difficult.

This idea of a birdcage as a visual to understand something so abstract and almost invisible as the system of oppression has been priceless to me. It gives voice to something that, because we all are within it, can be hard to understand. Without understanding, how do we move the conversation forward to improve the experiences of everyone? For this reason, I am grateful for Frye's insight.

I believe this idea of the birdcage correlated to the system of oppression was the deeper implication of Maya Angelou's I Know Why the Caged Bird Sings. When I read that book for the first time in junior high school

---

[1] Full article in Appendix

the concepts and feelings resonated on a deep level. As a white-skinned Native American, I understood what was being said and what was left unsaid in those pages.

I was first introduced to this idea of the "Cage of Oppression" in my training as an anti-oppression trainer in the 1990s through Cultural Bridges to Justice[2]. My own integration of the powerful tool as represented by joan olsson in 1988 was the model that allowed me to begin to synthesize information within social justice work as well as neuroscience, social psychology, LEAN[3], education, and more.

The Cage became a core component of how I saw the problems *and solutions* of the system of oppression. It is a way to present information, without shame or blame, from the 30,000-foot view down to the personal view, from the macro to the micro, in a way that people willingly learn and develop tools and strategies to move themselves forward.

I know that one of the barriers to change in the areas of social justice is the "cart before the horse" or, as discussed in the Introduction, starting in the middle of the conversation. People are expected to see things differently, have conversations, and make changes within themselves and the groups they belong to without having the tools or skills with which to do so. The Cage became the vehicle by which I could right the horse and cart.

I have to say, it wasn't a conscious do-it-now decision. It unfolded over time as I found myself synthesizing more information and coming back to the Cage to explain it, first to myself and, ultimately, to others.

I have since expanded and expounded on the Cage of Oppression framework, using it as a foundational premise in all the work I do. I have

---

[2] https://culturalbridgestojustice.org/

[3] Lean Learning is the Learning & Development (L&D) process of getting the right learning, to the right audience, at the right time, in the right quantity to achieve perfect work flow, while minimizing waste and being flexible to change.

developed physical activities that have profound abilities to really show people (as in, you can literally see what I'm talking about) how the system of oppression works and impacts themselves, groups to whom they belong, and groups to whom they don't belong. It helps to answer common questions and allows people to find their own answers. Best of all, it is a starting point that has the potential of putting people in a common, unthreatening space as we embark on social justice conversations *together*.

That's what is in this text, the beginnings and foundational explanations of The Cage of Oppression. Understanding the Cage allows us to see between the bars – which is where it gets interesting and promising. I'm offering my window view of how people can "play nicely in the sandbox" while honoring who they are, what they think and believe, and how they see the world – both individually and collectively.

This is the journey through respect that intertwines with belonging that ultimately lands us all in a place of justice and dignity = equity.

This is, in my tradition and perspective, work we *all* need to do. As individuals, we find a way so that, collectively, our organizations and governments really are safe places where we all belong, live, and thrive.

I'm so glad you have chosen to join me on this journey.

Context of Content

Warning label.

First and foremost, and I will repeat this often, **the Cage of Oppression is a systemic view of oppression**, from above, in the stratosphere, looking at it as a whole and a collective, a macro view. It simplifies the complexities of history, interactions, social conditioning, expectations, and so much more. The gift is that of simplicity. It provides us a visual representation to manage and manipulate, to explore and extrapolate. The system it represents is not, however, finite. The tool, though, gives us the chance to take ideas and concepts apart concretely to consider the infinite impacts, meanings, and messages.

Because it is the 30,000-foot view, to best understand it initially, *you will need to resist the urge to see yourself in it*. The individual experience can be explored as the micro of the Cage, but not until we fully understand the framework, as a whole, with its full implications and intricacies as a *system*.

Origins

For whatever reason, for the last several thousands of years, humans seem to have a need for hierarchy. Someone needs to be in charge, at the top. Someone also needs to be at the bottom. As a result, every country has its own systemic Cage. The -isms, groups, and conversation might be different but the system of oppression exists in all countries.

The framework discussed here is built on the experience within the United States.

The origination of this country's Cage was the Founding Fathers. Note it was not the Founding Parents. This is relevant because the Cage was built on the experience of those who created it. Its creation was simultaneously intentional and unintentional.

Remember, the Founding Fathers came from a Cage. They arrived here trying to escape a Cage that didn't work for them. Consequently, they tried to improve on the Cage they knew, but for their own best interest. This is the reason the foundations of the Cage, the "privilege trifecta," is about race, gender, and class. The Founding Fathers created their systems, the foundations of our government systems, on the success of white, men, who owned land (wealth).

These were the parameters for the right to vote. This was the top of the hierarchy.

Women and slaves were property. Natives were savages. None could own land.

This was the beginning. This is the context under which the Cage then progressed and grew. We now have more -isms that we can name and many more we probably can't. The ones represented in our framework are the eight most common and easy to identify.

It exists

We have data that supports the existence of the system of oppression. That is a fact.

Whether we look at education, law enforcement and the justice system, poverty, health care, real estate, politics, or census demographics the data points to those who have access and opportunity and those who don't. That data reflects systemic oppression. If you'd like to look at that data yourself, google the industry you're interested in and "disparities data" or "disaggregated demographic disparity data".

What we are doing with the Cage here is trying to represent that system of oppression in a way that allows us to better understand the impacts, talk about our individual and group experiences, and move forward in a different way. In my presentation of the framework, I aim to neutralize the shame and blame and explore realities and the possibilities of altering realities.

Vocabulary

The most important part of creating a common experience (The Cage) we first need to have common vocabulary.

There are a lot of words we use all the time but don't mean the same thing. You will see a lot of those words below. But I want to start with what, for me, is the most important word to understand, RESPECT.

This is a word that can carry a lot of variation based on where we come from, who are People are, what groups and communities we belong to, and exactly how and when we use the word. Since it's the name of my business (With Respect LLC) it is important that I define what I mean by this word. It is best summed up in this graphic.

Remember
Equity
Sincerity
Patience
Empathy
Compassion
Truthfulness

RESPECT

Our working definition of RESPECT is

Remember to actually pull it out of the back of our brain and use it.

Equity. This is not the idea of equal. It is the idea of Justice, getting what we need, maintaining our human rights.

Sincerity. Say what you mean, mean what you say.

Patience. This is the art of waiting, with heart. There are many types of patience, the type required to stand in line or be in traffic and the kind that is needed to support another's learning and growing, even when it isn't as fast yours or when it doesn't happen exactly as you think it should.

Empathy. The ability to relate to the feeling of another, not because the experience is the same, but because we are all emotional beings.

Compassion. This is the action of empathy. If my neighbor's mother dies, I know how it feels when I am grieving (empathy) and so I want to do something kind like make a casserole or send flowers.

Truthfulness. This differs from honesty. Honesty can be brutal. Truthfulness speaks its truth in a way that can be heard. My best example is if there is a giant car-eating hole down a specific street and I want to help cars not get eaten, I may very well stand on the corner, yelling my warning. If I am in a country that speaks Mandarin and I am yelling in German, very few cars will be spared.

Keep in mind this is my definition, my expression of respect, my perspective. But you're going to hear the word a lot. It's important you know what I mean by it. The same is true of the rest of the words defined below.

I really encourage you to review them. Please don't skip over them thinking you know what they mean. These are words commonly used, and as I discussed earlier, we don't always share a common understanding of what we mean when we use those words.

ALLY. One whose personal commitment to dismantling oppression is reflected in a willingness to educate oneself about oppression, challenge one's own prejudices, learn and practice the skills of anti-oppression, interrupt oppressive remarks, behaviors, policies, and institutional structures. An ally does not speak for or over, is not a position of stature or virtue signaling, nor is it a self-assigned label. Allyship is a lifestyle that seeks to recognize first their own position of privilege and second finds ways to interrupt the system of oppression. Most people in their experience of intersectionality are positioned to be an ally *and* to need an ally.

BELONGING. The human emotional need to be an accepted member of a group. It is a human right of being an essential part of something.

CODE SWITCHING. The practice of moving back and forth between two language variations or cultures; the ability to adapt behavior and language to varied situations based on context of who is present and what is going on.

CULTURE. "Culture is who we are and who we are becoming. It is the food we put on the table, the way we cook it, the utensils in which we eat it, the relations between the people who sit at the table and the people who cook and serve, what is done with the leftovers, what is discussed during the meal, what music, dancing, poetry or theatre accompany it, and the social and spiritual values of those present - for when we say culture, we include the visions, dreams, and aspirations of humanity." ("The Power of the Word: Culture, Censorship and Voice." Women's World, 1995)

DISCRIMINATION. An ACT. A failure to view all persons equally where no reasonable distinction can be found between those favored and those not favored (Blacks Law Dictionary). A showing of partiality or prejudice in treatment; specific policies or actions directed against the welfare of a group.

DIVERSITY. The uniqueness of individuality that is used to group people together; race, ethnicity, age, ability, gender, gender identity, socio-economic status, sexual preference, physical appearance, religious perspective, political ideology, learning style, communication style, life experience... It is important to avoid dividing people based on diversity. Instead, celebrate the strengths and opportunities that each brings to the table and use those strengths to build a community where everyone feels and knows they are welcome, equal, respected, and belong.

ENTITLEMENT. The conscious or unconscious feeling and behavior that you have the right to do or have what you want without having to work for it or deserve it, just because of who you are.

ETHNICITY. Belonging to a social group that has a common national or cultural tradition.

ETHNOCENTRIC. Evaluating other peoples and cultures according to the standards of one's own culture.

EXPLICIT BIAS: Prejudice – A PRE-JUDGEMENT based on myth, missing information, assumptions, and sometimes, personal experience.

GASLIGHTING. A specific type of manipulation where the manipulator is trying to get someone else (or a group of people) to question their own reality, memory or perceptions. When there is harm caused, the manipulator may also blame the one harmed for their own pain.

HISTORICAL TRAUMA. This refers to cumulative emotional and psychological wounding, extending over an individual lifespan and across generations, caused by traumatic experiences. There is evidence of DNA impact, that traumatic events can get recorded in DNA and passed down to the next generation. There's a field of study now called epigenetics in medicine and psychiatry observing this phenomenon and how it can be addressed therapeutically.

IMPLICIT BIAS: Hard-wired brain pathways that are designed as our risk assessment. They are attitudes, beliefs, or assumptions that affect our understanding, actions, and decisions in an unconscious manner including favorable or unfavorable perspectives activated involuntarily without intentional control that become pervasive, distinct mental constructs that are malleable and acted on without awareness. They interfere in our lives when they don't align with our self-identification or desires in our behavior or beliefs.

INTERNALIZED DOMINATION. A form of internalized oppression where there is an underlying acceptance of the dominant culture as superior, resulting in feelings of superiority, self-righteousness, guilt, fear, projection, and denial of reality. This effects individuals with both privilege and target experiences.

INTERNALIZED OPPRESSION. The process by which individual comes to accept and live out the inaccurate myths and stereotypes applied to a target group resulting in the normalization of oppression. This effects individuals with both privilege and target experiences.

INTERSECTIONALITY: The impact of target on privilege and privilege on target in an individual. It is the "crossing of the bars" that creates a unique individual experience of the system of oppression.

MICROAGGRESSION. A small act or remark that makes someone of a target group feel insulted or treated badly because of their race, sex, etc. (target experience) even though the act or remark may not have been intended or understood by the non-target. These do, as single acts/remarks or a series over time, cause emotional harm.

OPPRESSION. A system of structured dis-equality where the goods, services, rewards, privileges and benefits of the society are available to individuals according to their presumed membership in social identity groups. This system of dis-equality or dis-equal allocation of resources is supported and reinforced by the power structure (money, military, police, etc.) of the society. (Barbara J. Love, 1994. "Understanding Internalized Oppression.")

Prejudice + Discrimination + Systemic Power = Oppression

POLITICALLY CORRECT. A tool of privilege used to define appropriate, descriptive language for marginalized and target populations that minimizes guilt and reduces access to personal awareness of implicit bias, that is seldom created with the input of "those people".

PRIVILEGE. Choices, entitlements, advantages, benefits, assumptions, and expectations *granted based on membership in the culturally dominant group.* Privilege group membership is usually determined at birth: white child, male child, child born into economic security, child born without a disability, etc. It includes the privileges granted by society, as well as the assumptions and expectations internalized by people in the privileged and target groups.

PREJUDICE. A PRE-JUDGEMENT based on myth, missing information assumptions, and sometimes, personal experience.

PULL-DOWN EFFECT. Also known as "crab bucket syndrome" is often used to describe social situations where one person is trying to better themselves and others in the community attempt to pull them back down.

RACISM. Oppression (prejudice + discrimination + systemic power) based on the variation of skin color from the dominant culture. It is the assumed superiority that grants the right to dominate - exclude, discriminate against, abuse, hate, kill. NOTE: any form of oppression - classism, heterosexism, sexism, et al, can be substituted. (Adapted from the work of Audrey Lorde)

SOCIAL CONDITIONING. The norms and ideologies that we adopt from the society around us about self, education, employment, culture, religion, spirituality, relationships, safety, other people, and family life

STEREOTYPE. A GENERALIZATION imposed on an entire group based on a real or perceived characteristic of some individual belonging to that group, or based on a cultural norm which has been distorted, or based on a myth or total misunderstanding of the group/ethnicity/culture.

TARGET. Another term for marginalized populations or minorities.

VIRTUE SIGNALLING. Also called "humbragging," it is self-glorifying behavior that serves as an attempt to show other people that you are a good person, for example by expressing opinions that will be acceptable to them, especially on social media

---

I want to pull forward some important concepts and definitions that help to make a few things very clear.

Stereotype.   A GENERALIZATION.

Prejudice.   A PRE-JUDGEMENT.

Discrimination.   AN ACT (behavior, action, etc)

Let me give you a benign example of the above.

Let's say I believe the generalization (stereotype) that broccoli causes cancer. I now have a pre-judgement (prejudice)that broccoli is bad for me. You invite me to dinner and serve broccoli. I display an act (discrimination) of not eating the broccoli and, potentially, lecturing you on the perils of broccoli.

These three words (stereotype, prejudice, discrimination) define the process we all fall prey to;

1. the development of opinions and ideas that are based on stereotypes,
2. that lead to prejudice, that,
3. when we act on those prejudices, become active discrimination.

All of us do this. It is part of social conditioning (see Chapter 6).

When we now look at the word oppression, we recognize these foundations of stereotype, prejudice, and discrimination. **The difference, however, is the addition of systemic power.** This is an extremely important concept to remember as we explore the Cage.

"The root of the word 'oppression' is the element "press."
The press of the crowd; pressed into military service; press a
pair of pants; press the button."

"Presses are used to mold things or flatten them or reduce
them in bulk, sometimes to reduce them by squeezing out the
gasses or liquids in them. Sometimes pressed is something
caught between or among forces and barriers which are so
related to each other that jointly they restrain, restrict, or
prevent the thing's motion or mobility. Synonyms include
mold, immobilize, reduce."

"The experience of oppressed people is that of the living of
one's life is confined and shaped by forces and barriers
which are not accidental or occasional and hence avoidable,
but are systemically related to each other in such a way as to
catch one between and among them and restrict and penalize
motion in any direction. It is the experience of being caged
in: all avenues, in every direction are blocked or booby trapped."[4]

The Cage of Oppression

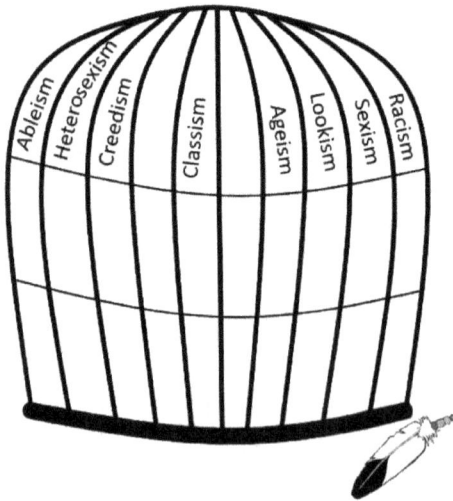

Ableism, Heterosexism, Creedism, Classism, Ageism, Lookism, Sexism, Racism

The Cage is the visual representation of the system of oppression. Starting to see it?

---

[4] Marilyn Frye. "Oppression." The Politics of Reality, 1983

Diving In!

Let's talk about the nuts and bolts of the image itself.

Another quick reminder (I told you I'd say it often) that this is a *systemic* view, the macro perspective. For right now, do everything you can to resist seeing yourself (or others) in it. That comes later. Just follow this overview to understand what it is this framework shows us and the foundations from which we can learn more.

Notice first that it has vertical *bars* and horizontal *tiers*. This language is important so I can talk about the framework in this flat 2-dimensional environment. I'm used to being able to point and draw on it, so bear with me as I improvise to make things as clear as possible.

The Cage of Oppression

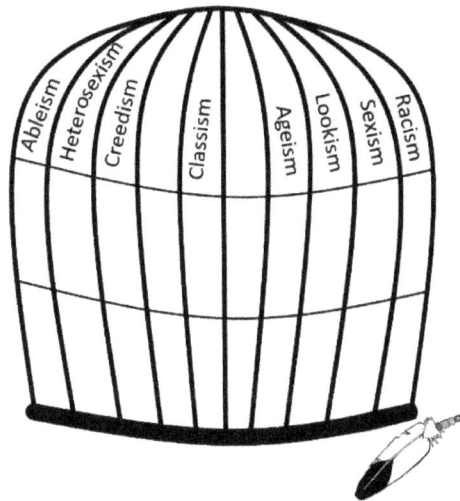

The top tier is the "-isms," the listed oppressions. The eight that are highlighted here are the most prominent, the ones we talk about or that can be recognized more readily. While it may be obvious to some, I will say, this is not an exhaustive list. There is lots of room for conversation of what other -isms might be included.

The Cage of Oppression

Now, in the second image, we note that the middle tier is identified as that of Privilege.

Reminder of our definition of privilege.

Privilege is defined as choices, entitlements, advantages, benefits, assumptions, and expectations granted based on membership in the culturally dominant group.

Privilege group membership is usually determined at birth, often unrecognized by the members in the same way fish would have trouble defining water. It includes the privileges granted by society, as well as the internalized assumptions and expectations by those within and outside the privilege group.

Clearly, this is the tier that holds the groups that experience privilege in current US society. This tier is that of the dominant cultural group and consequently is the *culture of power*. It is the groups withing that tier that make the majority of the decisions for the rest of the Cage. This connects back to the Founding Fathers and our conversation of origin of the Cage.

Remember the definition of oppression? It requires systemic power. Again, the groups identified within the Cage in the Privilege tier are the culture of power, the systemic power.

The bottom tier is identified as that of Target, **the term used to identify historically marginalized groups**. This is the tier of the oppressed.

It is a good time to point out that everyone is in the Cage. Whether a group is in the privilege tier or the target tier, they are all inside it, impacted by it, unable to escape. There is no more shame or blame in being born into a privileged group then there is in being born in target group.

The Innards

It's time to get to the inside of the Cage. Note in the third image, there are words in between the bars and tiers. This is the defining of the groups identified by the -isms by their privilege and target.

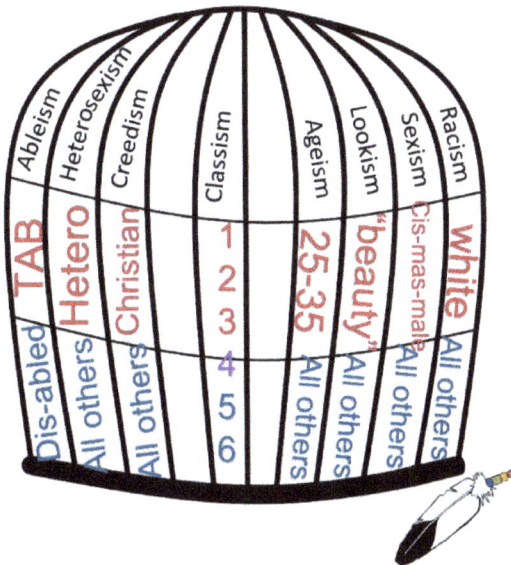

The Cage of Oppression

We will start to the far left with **Ableism**. The acronym in the privilege tier is TAB. That represents Temporarily Able Bodied. The language within the Cage is important. Ableism is one of the oppressions where individuals can move across the bar that divides privilege and target.

For example, if you are today able-bodied but step off a curb and get hit by a bus and tomorrow are in a wheelchair, you will move across the bar and become an individual who experiences a dis-ability. Consequently, TAB identifies the privileged group of this -ism.

Speaking of the use of language, notice that the word dis-abled is hyphenated. It is a way to delineate the idea that people are NOT disabled; they experience a disability. Differentiating is a way to avoid using the Cage framework to continue oppression of target populations. The full phrase "experiences a disability" didn't fit inside the small box of the image so I created a shorthand that I could then explain.

Understanding this oppression is about awareness, the lack of which emphasizes privilege. Unless you yourself or someone you are close to uses a wheelchair or scooter, it is easy not to notice the number of barriers to access there really are, particularly in older buildings and communities. My own experience with a service dog has allowed people who, upon spending time with me in public, begin to realize the prejudice and ignorance that can challenge a simple lunch out.

Hopefully, you're doing well not seeing yourself or other individuals in the box (even though I used an individual example to define TAB and explain the impact). These are two groups of people – those who are temporarily able-bodied and those who experience a disability.

To the right of Ableism, we find **Heterosexism.** This is about sexual identity and who we love. The privilege group is those people who identify as heterosexual or straight. In our current culture, the very top of the privilege group tends to be straight couples, a man and a woman. The target group is all other sexual identities and orientations. While the LGBTQ acronym commonly comes to mind, please note there are many more identities within the target communities that are not represented.

Language is important to me, so I want to make note that the general "all others" in this Cage image is about lack of space, not lack of respect, and in no way is meant to slight or further oppress target populations. If you find this to be a microaggression, I encourage you to reach out to me on Facebook or LinkedIn for a meaningful conversation.

The next category is **Creedism**. This is about religion. In the United States, Christianity is the dominant religion. All other religions, non-religions, and spiritualities are in target. The best, less politicized example of this oppression is the recognized national holidays and their direct alignment with Christian celebrations and, perhaps more importantly, the missing national recognition of other religious holidays.

Creedism has other tiers within the target experience. Specific religions with a history of oppression include Antisemitism & Islamophobia. We see federally recognized holidays stemming from Christian origins. Other religious holidays, while gaining in awareness, don't hold the same prestige in time off of work or national celebrations. This makes clear that, despite the idea that the United States was founded on the premise of religious freedom, the history of the country is steeped with the contrary.

Checking in to help remind you that this is the 30,000-foot view. Stay out of individualizing it. Good job!

Next, right in the middle, is **Classism**. This is about wealth. You will notice that this column is divided into six numbers (with further delineations possible). That's because this is a prime example of how within privilege and target there are often additional tiers. The longer I live the more tiers classism seems to take on. The numbers are used to show you where the categories, discussed below, fall in privilege and target. One through three are red indicating they are the privileged groups. Five and six are blue indicating they are the target groups. Four is purple because, as we will discuss, it is where the line gets crossed.

One. This is what has become known as the 1%. This is the uber-wealthy.

Two. This is the wealthy or affluent. This group most often inherited their money and the money will remain in the family lines.

Three. This is the upper middle class. Most of this group have earned their money within their own lifetime.

Four. This is middle class. We are, for the sake of the Cage image, dividing middle class into two parts; those with assets and those without assets. Those with assets (stocks, bonds, IRAs, offshore accounts, insurance policies, etc.) experience privilege. Those without assets might be doing okay – for now. This is the working poor, a target experience. This is part of the conversation related to the "vanishing middle class."

Five. This is those who are poor. They live below the defined line of poverty for this country but it isn't necessarily where they or their families came from. They may have been middle or even upper middle class and something happened to their assets that caused them to lose it all. We still see those who were impacted by the recession in 2008, joined by the recent economic impacts, in this group.

Six. This is generational poverty, made up of those who have not ever had money or whose money was taken as part of the system of oppression.

Classism is in the middle of the Cage for a reason. Statistically, this is the -ism that defines success by society's standards. It can be one of the biggest factors in the impact of privilege and target across other -isms (something we will explore further in the chapter on intersectionality). Additionally, class and race cannot be easily teased apart.

Both Black and Native communities experience higher than average poverty. This is not by accident.

Consider that when Native Americans were relegated to reservations, they weren't given the best of the land, adequate resources, or access to what could have allowed tribes to thrive. This was the direct result of the racism that viewed/s Native Americans as savages and less than human (remember, census data does not reflect Natives as one whole human until 1956).

Similarly, when slaves were emancipated, they weren't given money, land, or support to make a new, thriving life. Again, this is the direct result of the racism that viewed/s Blacks as less than human (they were counted as one whole human in the census by 1870).

Both of these communities, as well as others of color, when they gain(ed) assets, often had/have them subsequently taken by force. We still see the impact of those systemic choices today on the economic and cultural development of these communities.

Still with me on the 30,000-foot view? Remember we are discussing groups, not individuals.

Moving to the right, we find **Ageism**. This is the discrimination of youth and elders. In the United States the age band of privilege is about 25 years old to 35 years old.

Those who present as female experience the privilege sooner. This plays out in media and culture as all the creams, gadgets, and potions designed to keep women looking young and the idea of a younger woman on an older man's arm. Those who are male presenting experience the privilege longer. Consider the idea of how a man with graying hair is described as "distinguished." This is where we find an example of intersectionality where one ism is impacted by another. We will talk about that further in Chapter 6.

Ageism highly impacts individuals in areas such as healthcare, money and wealth, and employment. Forty is a magic number where it becomes more difficult to be hired, particularly in a lateral or elevating career move, especially for women.

The target population for ageism is those who are either younger than 25 and older than 35.

Lookism is our next bar over. This is the sense of beauty. We all grow up being conditioned for beauty. It's why you find lawns that are cut to a few inches and edged well to be aesthetically pleasing and why we all fawn over pictures of sunsets and sunrises. It is significant to note that this is a more malleable ism, however, meaning it changes over time. For example, in the 1950s to early 60s Marilyn Monroe was the epitome of beauty. She was a size 14. Cameron Diaz, identified as one of the most beautiful women in the US in 2022, is a size 4.

The privilege group in lookism are what we know as "beautiful people." Airbrushing in media has made some of that beauty standard unobtainable yet the commercial industry continues to market to that impossible standard. While the standard of beauty has a marked impact on women, men are not immune and have standards established for them as well.

The target population for lookism is anyone who is not considered beautiful. This is the box of the Cage that we see the highest impact of bullying. Bullying often targets those who look different, outside of the norm and what is accepted as beautiful. Those in many of the target groups have visual differences (those who experience a disability or poverty, those who aren't straight, religious dress or symbolism). This creates a level of intersectionality within lookism. For example, if I wear hand-me-down clothes that are stained (the result of a poverty experience) I may find myself the victim of unkind remarks and potentially even physical violence because I don't look the "right way."

30,000-foot view, right?

Moving to the right, we find ourselves at **Sexism**. The younger generations might rename this bar *genderism*, as the spectrum of gender continues to expand. Regardless of what we call it, the privilege group doesn't change.

The very top tier of the privilege group is the cis, masculine, male. Cis means you align in your gender identity with the anatomy with which you were born. In this case, it is male. Masculinity is a concept used to define maleness in our culture. The more masculine, the more privilege. Those males who are less masculine to effeminate have a different experience, though it is still privileged.

The target group here is all other gender identities.

Our last move takes us to **Racism**. This is probably the ism that has had the most attention lately. The privilege population is White with the target population that of all shades of Black and Brown people.

How did you do with staying in the systems' view of the Cage of Oppression?

Why a Cage?

You now understand what the Cage of Oppression framework is, but why the *Cage* of Oppression.

1. We are *all* inside the cage. While our experiences are different, we are *all* trapped inside the Cage, as individuals, as members of different groups (chosen and unchosen), and as a collective society. This is relevant and important as we comprehend the impact of the system of oppression and how it affects us all, each and every one of us. It also helps explain why some of us don't see the impact on ourselves and/or others. Consequently, as we explore solutions and opportunities of dismantling the Cage, none of us is outside of it nor do we escape it.
2. As we discussed in the explanation of the Cage, it has bars and tiers within the bars. This visual is useful in integrating the realities of the experience within those tiers, across the bars, and throughout the Cage. This is one of the reasons it is such a great tool; it allows us to see the separations and begin to ask ourselves how best to blur the bars. As we explore translation points and allyship, this becomes a powerful tool to support our exploration and consideration.
3. Cages cannot be dismantled by removing a single bar. You must dismantle the entire cage to successfully eliminate it. This is true of the system of oppression. It cannot be dismantled by trying to remove a single -ism. In fact, just as in a ball of yarn that has been tangled and knotted, if you pull on one string, you actually make the knots tighter and the mess worse. The same thing happens within the Cage.

I can hear some of you resisting or doubting the framework. Let's explore resistance for a moment.

Resistance, in my experience and research, manifests from one of two motivations: learning or fear.

As a learning modality, people use resistance to bang what they are learning against what they already know. In the learning framework we will explore later in this book, it is what we call *discord*. Resistance as part of the learning process asks questions like:

- Yeah, but...
- What about <this> or <that>?
- It isn't true <here>, is it?
- But there's this <other research/perspective>. Have you considered that?
- How can that be true if <this> is true too?

In this sense, it isn't true resistance because it is looking for a way to comprehend and integrate the new information. It is part of moving forward in the learning process.

Resistance as fear is different. It stems from a core need for safety and survival. It happens when what we are learning feels threatening to who we believe ourselves to be, what we believe, or our world view. Safety is a valid need and when it is missing, individuals have the right to air their concerns. Creating psychological and physical safety for these learnings and conversations is a mechanism to be able to continue forward in the learning process avoid using the fear as an excuse to prevent us from moving forward in the learning process.

In my experience, this is the resistance in people who have been in a learning environment (mostly on the topic of "diversity") that has left them feeling shame, blame, guilt, or judgement. This explains why much of fear resistance comes from those who experience privilege, particularly one or more of the trifecta of privilege; Racism, Sexism, and Classism.

While we will talk about this more later, recognizing this type of resistance as a fear response allows us to stay in a place of compassion.

I have seen this resistance show up in language like:

- That's bullsh**!
- No one can cage another in.
- This is teaching helplessness.
- That's just people playing the victim role
- You're a Marxist!
- Seems a handy excuse to keep people from owning their mistakes
- This just keeps people from trying

The best techniques I use to support positive outcomes for this type of resistance is head on, with compassion. I don't go tit-for-tat, responding to their claims and statements. I remind them that this is a systemic framework, the 30,000-foot view and I need them to resist the urge to put themselves inside the Cage right now. That's why they feel threatened; they personalize the Cage. Remember, first and foremost, the Cage represents the *system* of oppression. The individual experience inside it is totally different.

I ultimately ask them if they can bear with me, be open to learning with me, and we can talk about their thoughts as needed after we learn more together, encouraging them to use time during a break or after the session. Most often this allows the group process to move forward. It also serves most of the learners to really be able to take in the information and settle into the framework more comfortably.

It doesn't mean I don't answer their earnest questions. It's just that there is nothing I can say in this moment that will calm their fear. I have to depend on my ability to engage them throughout the content in a way that allows them to change their experience.

Another helpful way to look at resistance comes from Rick Maurer's work, <u>Change Without Migraines</u>.[5]

---

[5] https://rickmaurer.com/articles/resistance-to-change-why-it-matters/

Maurer identifies three tiered, categorical reasons for resistance to change:

1. I don't get it,
2. I don't like it, and
3. I don't like you.

His article explains each and gives some good advice for managing resistance through that lens.

If you are experiencing your own resistance right now, I ask you to bear with me, stay in the learning within this text (keep reading), and invite you, as needed, to engage with me online (Facebook or LinkedIn).

Power

I'd like to take a moment to explore the concept of power a little deeper. As previously mentioned, the tier of privilege within the Cage of Oppression represents the Culture of Power. Exactly what does that mean?

Reminder: this is a continuation of the 30,000-foot discussion.

The groups that experience privilege are those within the system who make the rules and for whom the rules are most beneficial. We already talked about the idea that Native Americans and freed enslaved persons were not set up to financially succeed. It was by design. It isn't hard to see how that benefits the privileged groups of race and class.

Let's take a look at the lawmakers in this country. You will notice that the majority of them are white men, most of whom have been career politicians and have a relatively large accumulation of wealth. Who makes the laws in this country?

Look at healthcare. What gender and race are most doctors?[6] Did you know the patient framework for current medicine is the white male body?[7] Who is likely to get the better care?[8]

Looking at the financial industry. Who is it who pays the most in income taxes? Whose loan interest rates are highest? Who pays the majority of bank fees? The answer to each of these questions is the lower classes. Who, then, benefits?[9]

---

[6] https://www.webmd.com/a-to-z-guides/news/20210720/white-mens-grip-on-us-health-care-may-be-slipping

[7] https://www.sciencedaily.com/releases/2008/10/081015132108.htm

[8] https://healthadministrationdegree.usc.edu/blog/the-5-populations-in-need-of-better-access-to-healthcare/

[9] https://www.policylink.org/sites/default/files/BreakingTheCycle_0.pdf

This is the Culture of Power. Again, the privilege trifecta (race, class, gender) are leading the way in power and benefit. Going back to our conversation regarding the Founding Fathers, it comes as no surprise.

Keep in mind, this is *systemic* power. That's what is required to create oppression. This is what creates the tiers in the Cage.

The examples above embody systemic power: power is derived by belonging to a group that experiences privilege in our society.

Be careful here. We aren't talking about individual or personal power. We are talking about power that is assigned to those who experience privilege.

If, Henry, a white male executive walks into a board room for a meeting, everyone in that room recognizes this person has power. Henry's subordinates know their place and how they must code switch to talk with this higher up individual. Women, through their social conditioning align their expectations and behavior to defer to Henry. A brown/black individual likewise aligns with their socially conditioned expectations and behaviors. It all happens in a nanosecond and, for many, is unconscious.

But what about Henry? He may not perceive himself as having any more power in the meeting than anyone else. This is his individual experience. Regardless, the stage is set by the groups to whom he belongs.

Let's talk about Henry's ability to think he doesn't have any more power than those in the room. That's actually a reflection of his privilege. Those in the room who are, particularly, non-male and/or non-white can't afford to not understand their place and the importance of "staying in their lane." The cost is too high.

Also in play is positional power. Simply by being an executive, Henry has power.

But who in our social constructs historically has access to that positional power? Remember our example of Native Americans and freed slaves. Women and non-binary individuals have a similar experience, as do those across the target tier – those not part of the Culture of Power.

That's systemic power. It is assigned, unearned, and, for many, invisible.

Systemic power is important to understand as we move forward. It is the result of privilege. The system of oppression creates privilege, providing systemic power, leading to the Culture of Power.

From Inside the Cage

Intersectionality.
Intersectionality is the individual experience within The Cage of Oppression. Based on the definition provided earlier, it is **the impact of target on privilege and privilege on target in an individual. It is the "crossing of the bars" that creates a unique individual experience of the system of oppression**.

The concept of intersectionality has been used to categorically explain the exacerbation of multiple target experiences in one person. I am using it differently, as a word that describes everyone's experience within the Cage. It is how a white male can experience a high level of oppression, potentially higher than a black female if the difference is that he experiences poverty and she wealth (Remember our discussion about the impact of classism. It is one of the primary game changers.).

In my lifetime, I have met very few people who have an experience that includes every privilege group or, in contrast, every target group. The majority of people have experiences of both sides of the bar. Additionally, there are bars that can and do get crossed throughout your lifetime. Consider creedism and conversion into one or another religion which has the potential to allow you to cross the bar. If you have the honor of living long enough, you will cross the bar of ageism and, more than likely, ableism. So there is movement which also influences the ability of individuals to *only* experience either privilege or target.

Using the Cage of Oppression, I can show you my personal experience within the bars.

Notice the shape it creates. Notice where my positions of privilege are and where they aren't.

The Cage of Oppression

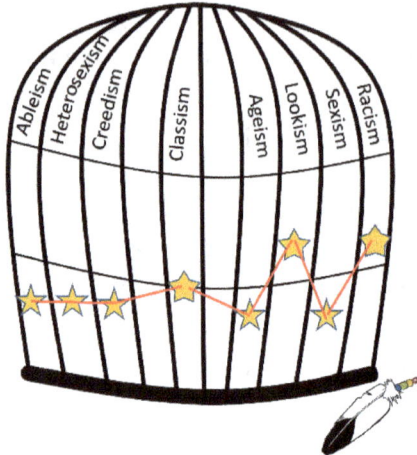

Based on this diagram, you know that I am a person who experiences a disability, I am not straight, I'm not Christian, I'm middle class, I'm not between the ages of 25-35 (though I once was), I'm average in appearance, I am not male, and I am white.

This experience is unique to me. I will tell you about my journey through and around the Cage later, but for now, you can see my individual experience within the it.

If we had eight points in a circle, each representing an -ism from the Cage, and we attached 3-d printing jets to them, we could create a shape based on the experience of target or privilege, much like what you see here only in 3-d. The shape each of us would end up with would be different. That's because no two people have the same experience within the Cage of Oppression. This is important in understanding how we can't judge an individual based on one -ism, what they look like, whether they look like us, or other ways of presenting. Each of the -isms is a facet of who we are. And remember, our framework of The Cage only has eight representational -isms. There are many more.

Similarly, there is no oppression olympics. It is not useful to try and determine who has been most oppressed, as groups or as individuals. This serves very little in the process of moving forward.

Don't confuse this with the importance of understanding history and the development of the Cage. The tendency in oppression olympics is to create a level of shame and blame that results in us versus them and very effectively stops conversation. The goal of understanding history and development is to deepen our understanding of the Cage to improve our opportunity to dismantle it.

Intersectionality shows us the shape of our experience within the Cage. As a tool to move forward, it also shows us where we as individuals need allies, and where we can be allies. There's an entire chapter dedicated to allyship, but for now, soak in that this is about using our intersectionality to create connection and movement that supports blurring the bars.

Implicit Bias

The human brain has over 180 hard-wired biases.[10] They are designed to, by and large, ensure our survival. These hard-wired biases operate without our awareness all the time, in nanoseconds. They are implicit biases. We are, therefore, all hard-wired with implicit bias.

 Here is the codex that lays out what we know about these hard-wired biases. If you're looking for a way to enlarge the image, google "brain bias codex" and you will find this image.

---

[10] 2018, Benson, Buster.

COGNITIVE BIAS CODEX

What Should We Remember?

Too Much Information

Need To Act Fast

Not Enough Meaning

DESIGNHACKS.CO · CATEGORIZATION BY BUSTER BENSON · ALGORITHMIC DESIGN BY JOHN MANOOGIAN III (JM3) · DATA BY WIKIPEDIA

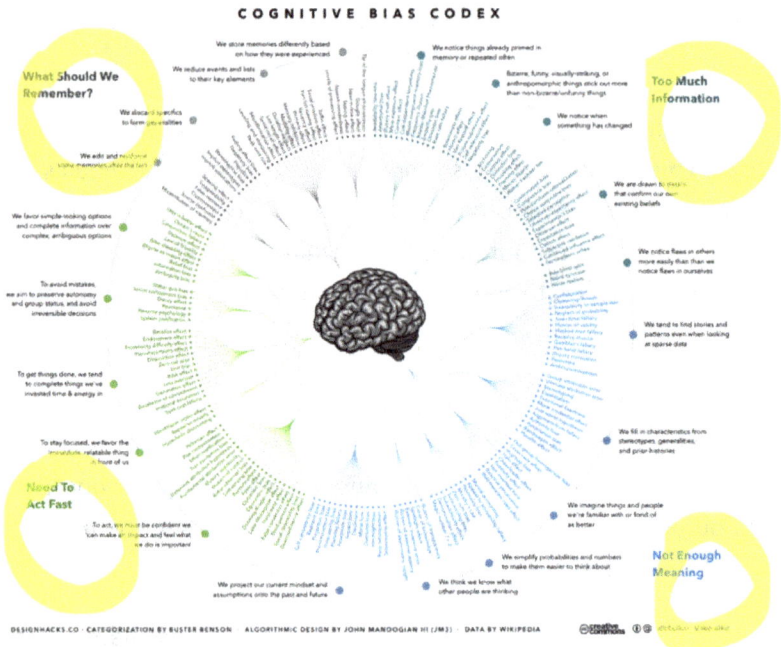

You will notice I've added highlights for the categories of the biases. They are

1. What should I remember?
2. What happens when there is too much information?
3. What happens if there isn't enough meaning?
4. What do I need if I have to act fast?

It's pretty easy to see how these four categories are directly related to survival.

Take it in for a few minutes: these are *hard-wired biases,* our *natural implicit bias*. Hold on to that thought

Next, let's discuss social conditioning. The definition offered at the beginning of the text is **the norms and ideologies that we adopt from the society around us about self, education, employment, culture, religion, spirituality, relationships, safety, other people, and family life**. This sounds benign. But consider the influences of social conditioning that cause us to recognize these "realities" in media.

Social conditioning includes stereotypes, learned rules of conduct, and even code switching. It includes the Cage.

Consider the colors used for Disney princesses. They tend to be light, pastels, soft.

What about the villains? Dark, sharp lines, deep colors.

What is the social conditioning that results? Consider the hard-wired **affinity bias** (we gravitate to those who look like us), **ingroup bias** (there is always a group that we know are the "in" group), and **social comparison bias** (comparing others to a social standard).

The result is I compare myself and those who look like me to that social standard of light is good and dark is bad. Am I part of the ingroup (light)? What about you?

Can you see how my natural implicit bias becomes overlayed by social conditioning, which is directly influence by The Cage?

What's the result?

Consider a woman walking to her car in a dark parking garage. She has someone walking toward her. Her hard-wired biases are now at work, but so is her social conditioning.

If the person walking toward her is a white male carrying a briefcase, her defensiveness probably reduces a bit (it's not eliminated). If it is a black man carrying a briefcase, her defensiveness probably increases.

Statistically, however, data doesn't support her implicit reaction. Most serial killers are white males.

Implicit bias is a survival mechanism. It is not inherently bad. When social conditioning, which is naturally influenced by the Cage, begins to entangle with and across our natural implicit bias, that's when we see things shift.

The question we ask ourselves is does the behavior I am exhibiting align with who I am and keeping myself safe. The internal bias that impacts me in such a way as to cause me to behave in a way counter to who I want to be is *negative implicit bias*.

Consider the following cartoon. You will notice that the implicit bias of each individual is influenced by their social conditioning. You can see the Cage represented within that social conditioning. What results is a risk assessment that determines their behavior.

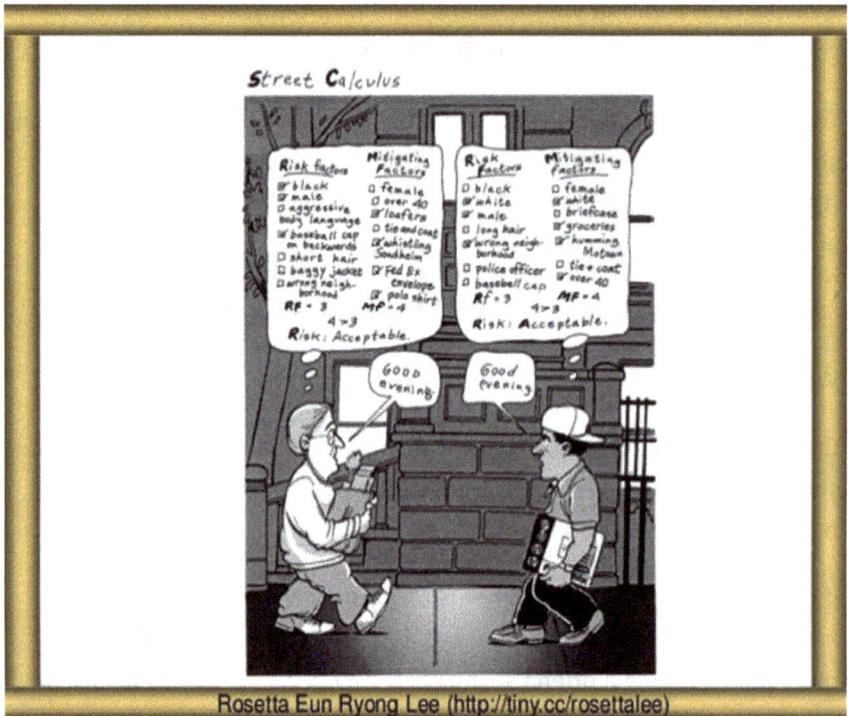

Rosetta Eun Ryong Lee (http://tiny.cc/rosettalee)

This is that impact of The Cage of Oppression that contributes to our social conditioning and, consequently, our implicit bias.

Based on where we find ourselves, within target and privilege, we learn our place in the Cage as part of that social conditioning. One of the best examples I can give comes from the work of Ruby Payne in her work exploring and explaining poverty. The chart below is my abridged synthesis of her hidden rules within classism.

TOPIC	POVERTY	MIDDLE	UPPER
Money	To be used, spent	To be managed	To be invested
Food	Did you have enough?	Did you like it?	Was it presented well?
Time	Now	Future	Past
Language	Casual register; for survival	Formal register; for negotiation	Formal register; for networking
Driving forces	Survival, relationships, entertainment	Work, achievement	Financial, political, and social connections

Can you see how much of the content is learned/socially conditioned? What is learned is based on your class, which is based on The Cage.

This shows us how the Cage influences our social conditioning and our implicit bias.

Again, social conditioning superimposed on our hard-wired biases = implicit bias. Implicit bias, in turn influences our behavior.

If my behavior doesn't align with my moral compass, beliefs, and/or values, then it is *negative* implicit bias. This is the implicit bias that I want to and can change.

There is an interesting study done by Goff & Jackson, published in 2014 (link is in the appendix). It found that the concept of innocence was removed from black boys earlier (age 10 years) than their white peers (age 14). The individuals who participated in the study had no idea they held beliefs that supported the premise. Yet they did. None of them intended it. They did not want it to be true about themselves. The evidence showed otherwise.

This is negative implicit bias. When it is brought to our attention, then we can choose to make the change. This is where tools become important.

Remember that's one of the historic barriers to success in making change in social justice; people don't have the tools. What tools do you have to recognize, challenge, and change your own implicit bias?

By the way, implicit bias is something that is virtually impossible to challenge alone or simply by reading books. We need other people from other experiences within the Cage to help us understand where our social conditioning and implicit bias lies. That's the catch 22 of the work. We need one another to successfully navigate and engage in the blurring of the bars.

Microaggressions

Implicit bias is the birthplace of microaggressions.

Remember that when we find ourselves acting on our implicit bias and making a comment or acting in a way that doesn't align with who we wish to be (negative implicit bias), we can choose to change it.

Our working definition of microaggression is **a small act or remark that makes someone feel insulted or treated badly because of their race, sex, etc., even though the insult, etc. may not have been intended, and that can combine with other similar acts or remarks over time to cause emotional harm.**

These are little comments or actions that are needle sharp, sometimes even causing a physical wince, facial response, or actual withdrawal. While they are by definition "small" the impact is in no way small. That's because they add up quickly and target groups experience them from cradle to grave.

Clarifying that microaggressions are directed toward target groups by privilege groups. Also reminding us that most of us have a varied intersectionality that includes both target and privilege.

In case you are wondering, rude comments from privilege to privilege or target to privilege is mean. It is not a microaggression but it isn't okay either. This is the gift of being clear with language; what *is* a microaggression and what *is not*. Just because it isn't a microaggression doesn't make it respectful or acceptable.

Microaggressions can appear covert. It might seem a benign comment about the uniqueness of ethnic hair or a compliment for a dress when it is actually one more layer of oppression, albeit a tiny-in-the-moment thing. But these tiny-in-the-moment things happen almost every moment for those in target groups. By the time adulthood is reached these aggressions no longer feel micro.

Microaggressions can develop from stereotypes.

Marc is a high school junior who identifies as Asian-American. He loves art and art history and enjoys developing his talents in painting and sculpting. His math teacher consistently criticizes Marc when he doesn't ace the tests commenting, "I'd expect more out of you, after all."

Angela is a young black woman who stands 6'. She loves to read and explore bookstores and libraries. Inevitably when she meets someone new, they ask whether or not she plays basketball. Angela shyly informs them she never even learned how to dribble a ball.

Morgan has been blind since birth. They are standing at the coffeeshop counter waiting for their order when a stranger walks up to them and tells them what an inspiration they are going out into the world despite their disability.

Micky is gender-fluid, working in a corporate environment. They enjoy trying out different clothing and styles, always professional but not always binary aligned as male or female. Several of Micky's colleagues consistently ask, "Are you a boy or a girl today? We're never really sure."

These are examples of *personalized* microaggressions. They are the things that individuals must endure, the result of implicit bias and privilege.

When people respond to the harm that they experience they are often met with "it was just..." This is the minimization of a painful experience and can be a form of gaslighting where the individual who is harmed is being manipulated to doubt their own perception, sometimes even blamed for their pain.

Microaggressions can be a systemic experience. Examples include

- a symbol such as a swastika or confederate flag
- catcalling and objectification of women as sex objects
- public prayer from a single tradition
- bathrooms without stalls and sinks that can be accessed from a wheelchair.

They can also be in the language we use:

- blackballing as an indication of outgrouping
- idioms like "bottom of the totem pole" and "send them down the river"
- disability – which literally means *not able*, like a car with a dead battery on the side of the road
- words like retard, spaz, deafmute, and cripple.

We see how the Cage and our position within it have direct ties to implicit bias and microaggressions. But that's not all.

Internalization

Internalized oppression and its twin, internalized domination, are intertwined with implicit bias and social conditioning *and* we all have them both.

In both, the word in common is internalized. Implicit bias is internalized. Social conditioning is internalized. They are intertwined and manifest as internalized oppression and internalized domination.

Internalized oppression is **the process by which individual comes to accept and live out the inaccurate myths and stereotypes applied to a target group resulting in the normalization of oppression. This effects individuals with both privilege and target experiences.**

Internalized domination is **a form of internalized oppression where there is an underlying acceptance that the dominant culture as superior, is normal and deserved, resulting in feelings of superiority, self-righteousness, guilt, fear, projection, and denial of reality. This effects individuals with both privilege and target experiences.**

It is important to note that both of these internalizations are experienced by the privilege and target groups because they are about the relationship (individually and systemically). That's what makes it work; we all have it. It's how we all play by the same rules.

This is one of the facets of The Cage that make it so hard to dismantle. The rules are embodied in every aspect of who we are as individuals and society. Like asking fish to define water, when you're standing in it, surrounded by it, living and breathing it, it becomes difficult to define, recognize, own, and change.

Let's see what we can do to wrap our brains around these concepts.

If I am in the target group, I internalize my own oppression *and* the domination over me of the privilege group. I learn how to behave, talk, and move through life in a way that minimizes the negative impact of my oppression. It is part of the encoding of my target position in the Cage. It is the invisible messaging that I respond to consciously and unconsciously.

Black parents teach their children how to behave with white people, particularly those in authority like teachers and law enforcement. Little girls are taught where they can be, who they can be with, what they should wear, how they should behave and talk, particularly around boys and men. This teaching is a survival tool. This is the behavior of internalized oppression. It is also the product of internalized domination. I am oppressed. You dominate.

While some of it is overt, there is a lot that is covert. I'm amazed at the number of my female friends who, when the server in a restaurant is male, their voice and behavior change. When I point it out, they argue with me that it even occurred.

Likewise, if I am in the privilege group, I internalize my own domination (I dominate) and the oppression of the target group (you are oppressed). The result is an expectation that, for example, as a male executive, my female secretary will get me coffee and be sure to bring it just the way I like it. It's also why I may overlook the highly qualified black woman for the promotion. When someone balks at my expectation, I am confused and may become defensive.

These are accepted norms in our culture. They are unspoken and invisible agreements across the bars and tiers of The Cage. Most of them are learned as young children and we don't even know they're in there. Sometimes it requires a jolt to remember that they're, not only there, but need to be changed.

Let's go back to Henry, our white, male executive. The reason those in the room see his power – whether he chooses to or not – is because of the internalizations of oppression and domination. When they each respond from their place of privilege or target, they are acting on those internalizations.

Henry's internalized domination means when a woman approaches Henry to compliment his leadership style, his response is to pat her hand and say, "That's so sweet of you to say. Thank you." He'd never have said that to a man.

Depending on her awareness and level of acceptance of internalized oppression/domination, she may very well accept his comment as normal.

In the event she responds differently, Henry may find himself in Human Resources' office trying to figure out what he did wrong. That's the internalized domination at play, leaving him blind to the privilege that surrounds him. But it is also influenced by his internalized oppression as well, his blindness to why the behavior he sees as "normal" for his interaction with women is not, contrary to his perspective, respectful

44

and open.

This makes clear the confounding nature created by the systemic experience of The Cage superimposed on the individual experience.

In other words, how natural implicit bias overlayed with the Cage results in negative implicit bias, microaggressions, internalized oppression, and internalize domination. This shows up in the intersectionality of the individual through thoughts, beliefs, behaviors, values, and language.

The view from inside the Cage isn't always as clear as we might like.

Allyship

Allyship is **one whose personal commitment to dismantling oppression is reflected in a willingness to educate oneself about oppression, challenge one's own prejudices, learn and practice the skills of anti-oppression, interrupt oppressive remarks, behaviors, policies, and institutional structures. An ally does not speak for or over, is not a position of stature or value signaling, nor is it a self-assigned label. Allyship is a lifestyle that seeks to recognize first their own position of privilege and second finds ways to interrupt the system of oppression. Most people in their experience of intersectionality are positioned to be an ally *and* to need an ally.**

Notice this says a whole lot more about a personal, internal journey than it does about an external expression of that journey. That's because allyship is a **lifestyle**, it is an act of solidarity. When used as a self-assigned label, it becomes virtue signaling.

"Being an ally" has become a watered-down version of the concept, more like a badge to wear than a true understanding of what is meant by the word. I'm not even sure it IS the right word. I'm open to a new one. Regardless, let me expand and explain what I mean with this word (giving you all the opportunity to help me find a new word!).

An ally is a member of a privilege group who

1. recognizes the Cage and its impacts and implications
2. recognizes their position in the Cage
3. recognizes they have negative implicit bias, internalized oppression/domination, and
4. that they engage in microaggressions and other language and behavior that support and reinforce the Cage.

With this realization, an ally makes the choice to

1. work on their own internalizations first

2. collaborates with member(s) of the target group
3. seeks to understand how they can best serve.

What can an ally do?

1. Listen to the story and demonstrate interest in the position of those you ally.
2. Stand behind them, physically and figuratively, when asked. Follow their lead.
3. Stand beside them when they need a position supported.
4. Open a door they can't and then step out of the way.
5. Say things they often cannot say.
6. Gain audience with a group they may not be able to reach and deliver the message they want that group to hear.

Guidelines for Allies.

- Listen to as many voices as possible to understand the core of any issue
- Educate yourself constantly. It's not the responsibility of those that you ally to educate you.
- Be flexible in your roles and transition when necessary.
- Speak up early, often, and always in the matter of inclusion and equality. You can't be an ally in isolation.
- Be open, honest, genuine, reliable, consistent, and willing to learn.
- True solidarity means supporting the work being done by those to whom you ally yourself. You are not creating a platform for your own voice or work. Turn the attention to those whose voices are often ignored.
- Be accountable. If you make a mistake, own it. Apologize and act differently moving forward.
- "Ally" is not a self-proclaiming identity. It is an act of solidarity.
- Being an ally is not a sometimes thing. Allies don't take breaks.
- Being an ally is not about being part of ingrouping.
- Don't speak for those for whom you ally yourself unless you have been asked.

Skills of an Ally.

- Authentic, mutual relationships
    - It is not a dog-and-pony show
- Acceptance
    - With personal boundaries
    - With confusion, misunderstanding, and conflict
- Listening
    - Listen to hear, not to speak
    - Suspend "The Judge"
    - If you feel compelled to respond, ask questions.
    - Seek clarity
- Respect
    - I don't need to know you, agree with you, or even like you to show you respect.
- Empower
    - Lead by example; stand in your power
    - Support new habits in self and those you ally.
    - Be willing to make mistakes.
- Clarity
    - In intention
    - In language
    - In role
    - In expectations

Because most of us also have the opportunity to seek and have an ally, it is important to remember when you have an ally:

1. They don't have all the answers.
2. It is okay for each of us to be as we are.
3. Allow for mistakes, be patient.
4. They don't understand everything, but they are willing to learn.

So how do allies find their place with those for whom they wish to provide allyship? I can speak from my own experience.

As a woman-owned business, there are organizations and contracts that

I would be hard pressed to secure on my own. Knowing that, I seek out male-owned businesses who do similar, good work and have the conversation. I am clear and upfront. It goes something like this:

> "We both know that I, as a woman-owned business, have a slim chance of securing this contract. You, on the other hand, as a male-owned business are much better positioned. If we work together, offering what you do and what I do, we offer them more. You, as the ally, lead the way through the door and together we can provide them with great services and move the organization forward where they want to go."

Seeking to be an ally requires the development of relationships, often one to one. Most important, are the conversations of privilege and target experiences shared to better understand where each has been and the desired outcome. When situations arise, if the request doesn't come, one can offer. Of course, the opportunity to hear "no" is always an option.

This is the advantage of common language; we can come together to have the conversations from a common place and clear intention. We know what we mean, what to expect, and how to deepen conversation because we know we are talking about the same thing.

My Story Inside the Cage

The idea of white privilege showed up in my life long before I realized it. That's true for most of us really. Before any of us knows it, we have benefitted – or not – from the color skin we were born into. No greater gift. No greater sin.

Then some of us become aware, before others, that something is different; something sets us apart. It's hard to put your finger on it as a young child. The words are there, the thoughts, the looks, the attitudes. But our innocent minds are still being formed, can't yet grasp what it all means.

Later, looking back, it becomes more obvious. The words we overheard, the actions we witnessed, the pain we experienced… It all begins to make sense as our lens of prejudice and privilege comes into focus.

That was my experience as the child of a Native American mother and an Appalachian white father.

Where it all began

The dark night comes into clear focus. My mother, Rose, was shot and killed in front of me. I was three years old. I could only watch in horror even as my older brother, himself only 5, cradled her head, pleading with her not to die. She died anyway.

I look to the assailant. My mind fogs with the realization that it is my father.

I did not understand the slur at the time, "Prairie n***** got too big for her britches."

Her body was removed, dumped somewhere, I learned later. No one ever noticed.

Then my older brother, Mattie, and sister, Patty, were stabbed for being in the wrong place at the wrong time and they were the wrong color. But I was left standing.

"Not her. Halfbreed looks white."

Their bodies too were dumped. Even though they were children, no one noticed. No one ever asked me where they had gone, never again mentioned their names. It was as if they had never existed. They were just dead Indians.

At the age of almost 7, I now understood that what I looked like was different. I understood my skin was "white" and that made me different, that made me hard to eliminate, that allowed me to survive. I felt guilty.

Noticing

I started to notice what was different about me – dressed in the same clothes, with the same barely legal behaviors as any of my friends and cohorts – still different.

No one followed *me* around Nordstrom's like they did my best (black) friend.

Even though I was in the same neighborhood, talking the same, looking the same, the white woman didn't hug her purse and hasten her pace when I got close. She did when my black teammate passed her on the same street. Funny thing is, back then, I was the one she should have feared.

I spent many a long hour listening to the white family drone on about how much better off they were; after all, they were poor, but they were WHITE.

As time moved forward, things played out differently for me in school. Even in that inner city school that warehoused us for a few hours each day, I was different than the majority of my peers. I was identified as "cute" and "mischievous" for oftentimes greater offenses than my not-so-white counterparts.

I remember the time I pulled a knife on a kid who tripped me in the hall. As I was dragged to the principal's by two large teachers, I knew this would mean I would be kicked out. Indeed, another girl a year younger had simply gotten into a shoving match the week before and she was down in juvie.

As I entered the principal's office, he smiled at me. "Getting yourself in trouble again, eh?"

This wasn't my first time here.

"I guess."

"I'm going to send you home today. Be back on Monday and leave the blade at home. You hear me?"

Shocked, I nod.

It was years later as I looked back, I recognized that I looked white. The younger girl the week before was not.

The leg up

As I grew, my awareness grew. I saw the prejudice and felt the pain of oppression for the poverty I experienced, for the fact that I grew up in a poor neighborhood, running drugs and guns in the "family business."

And then I realized I didn't want to inherit that family business. I saw my only escape was to get an education. No one in my family had graduated high school let alone thought of going to college. There was no support.

Still in high school, I turned to a teacher and a counselor, both white women. They saw me, gave me a dream of higher education and did everything they could to help me along. They told me what classes to take and guided me to teachers who cared a little more than others.

They helped me learn how to do the research for what career I wanted, what colleges I could attend, and what scholarships and aide I could apply for to make it all come together.

Interestingly, I had a volleyball teammate, a friend of sorts, who also wanted to go to college. I know because we talked about it in the locker room before games. I mentioned it to my mentors. They nodded and told me there were others who had similar dreams but I had the potential. There were only so many resources and they needed to focus on me because I had such a great shot at making it. I shouldn't let it take up any of my time.

I accepted their words. I also gave my classmate as much information as I could. Her family didn't speak English. I now understand that she and her family may not have been citizens. I don't know that and it shouldn't have mattered.

I do know she didn't have a library card (most of the resources we had to access were in the library in the references and microfiche sections – this was way before computers). She wouldn't get one. Looking back, maybe she couldn't get one.

She also had no one helping her get through the hoops – the ACT and the arrangements to take it and the scores having to be logged and collected, the application fees, the essays. I had support lowering those hoops for me, making them easy to jump through. No one even tried for her.

The leg out

I made it to college but fell in and out of it, balancing where I came from with who I was becoming. In one of the times I was out of college, I married my dealer (seemed like a good idea at the time!) and had two children. Those children became the motivation to REALLY change my life.

I left my abusive marriage, got clean, went on welfare AND went back to college. I saw a huge myriad of differences in that welfare office. As a single, white-looking woman, who had started college, I was given benefits that included childcare and a stipend for my books and transportation costs. Those were monumental in my success in graduating from college.

Having dinner at a neighbor's house, also a single mom, we were discussing our benefits. When I mentioned my childcare benefits, she stopped short.

"What?"

"What what?"

"How did you get childcare?"

"Told my worker I needed it so I could go to class."

"And they gave it to you?"

"Yeah. Why?"

"I can't get childcare."

"Have you asked for it?"

"Of course, I asked for it!"

"What'd they say?"

"They told me I couldn't have it."

"Tell you why?"

"No."

We talked further. She was trying to get into the same college I was in, looking for the same opportunity I had. She needed the extra support from welfare to work out the childcare, just like me. The worker had flat out told her no. No explanation. No reconsideration.

Did I mention she was a black, single mother?

I came to learn that NONE of my friends and acquaintances of color had childcare or were considered eligible for the college bound benefits from welfare. Many of them asked. Most of them gave up. They were shuffled into low level jobs that few of them kept. It was more lucrative to stay at home with their kids; at least they had food stamps and housing.

Even the process of getting (and staying) clean and sober was easier for me than for brown skinned women. I was blatantly told that I was statistically more likely to stay clean and sober than another woman who was black. I never saw that study, but the white female worker who told me about it believed it.

If the study is real, I do wonder whether it considers the variables of institutionalized racism and classism and the likelihood that resource availability is also based on what neighborhood you're in which is based on the color of your skin.

Just a coincidence, right?

Because of the leg up and out I received I was able to finish college, clean and sober.

I was able to find a job outside of the poverty I was born into; I was able to give my children a different life. I became an entrepreneur.

Why did I make it out? A couple reasons stand out in this story.

1. The color of my skin
2. The allyship of those two white middle-class women in high school.

The Cage is alive and well throughout my story. It still is.

How did you respond to my story?

For some people they find it a story of strength and courage, they may even find it inspiring. This is an unconscious recognition of the Cage. We know what it takes to overcome the challenges the bars and tiers of the Cage present to individuals. When someone succeeds despite their target membership, we know what it took. We internally understand the Cage.

This is significant for those times when we are confronted by doubt that the Cage exists, when we find ourselves talking to that fish trying to help them define water. This is the advantage of being able to see other perspectives between the bars.

My story is a big part of my "why" for doing this work. I want the World to be a better place, to the Seventh Generation. I hold a vision of the change we can create and the outcomes it yields.

I believe that what I do to you I do to me and what I do to me I do to you. We are all interconnected, in this together. I seek to light a path that allows us all to treat one another, ourselves, and all the other creature-beings on this planet with respect.

The Power of Language

We have seen how powerful it is to have common language. By being clear about our definitions and intentions with language our conversations deepen and our opportunities for authentic relationships increases.

This validates just how powerful words are and how they can change the impact and response from others. This awareness of the language we use and how we use it is crucial to the perceptions others have of us and themselves, consciously and unconsciously.

Shame, Blame, Guilt, & Judgement.

Our directive, corrective, and management language often includes words and phrases that reflect shame, blame, guilt, and judgement.

Examples of common phrases reflecting shame, blame, guilt, and judgement include some variation of:

- "Shame on you!"
- "Why would you do that?"
- "I can't believe you did that!"
- "I'm disappointed in you!"
- "How many times do I have to tell you?"
- "Why can't you remember?"
- "Did you really just do that?"
- "What did I tell you?"
- "Stop acting stupid/rude/obnoxious."
- "If you don't stop, then this will happen."
- "You brought this on yourself."

Brené Brown on "Speaking Shame"

"Shame derives its power from being unspeakable. That's why it loves perfectionists – it's so easy to keep us quiet. If we cultivate enough awareness about shame to name it and speak it, we've basically cut it off at the knees…. When we don't talk about how we feel and ask for what we need, we often shut down, act out, or both."

Shame phrases:

- You're so sensitive.
- I didn't realize you were so fragile.
- I didn't realize this was such an issue for you.
- You're so defensive.
- I guess I'll have to watch what I say around you.
- It's all in your head.
- You seem really hostile.
- Loser, lame, and weak.

Brutal honesty is another problem. It's usually shame, anger, fear, or hurt disguised as honesty.

RESULTS.

As the result of short and long-term exposure to shame, blame, guilt, and judgement language, people develop coping behaviors in an attempt to protect their self-esteem and self-concept.
These include:

- Defensive response, even with minor feedback.
- Explosiveness.
- Blaming.
- Lying.
- Deflecting.
- Fear of being wrong.
- Extreme shyness.
- Poor or inconsistent social skills.
- Withdrawal.
- Unhealthy relationship skills.
- Grandiose, arrogant, or self-centered.
- Hopeless, helpless.

Behavior driven by guilt, shame, blame, and judgement most often finds its way to resentment. Change from these lenses is seldom sustainable. These are feelings that don't lend themselves well to sustainability. Constructive behavior that creates change has to be built from a collective perspective of improvement for the good of all.

This language is engrained in most of us. We grew up hearing it, we have raised and taught this to our children.

I realized my own level of use of shame, blame, and judgement with my children when they moved out after high school. See, when they moved out so did "Not me!"

"Not me!" is a deflection. It is a way to dodge whatever bullet is coming your way. This was my children's response when I asked, "Who did this?" or "Whose turn is to take out the trash?"

I wish I had learned the alternatives earlier in their lives so that my language could be clearer. What are the alternatives?

Safe & Respectful Language

- **Ask questions**. ("Can you tell me what's going on?")

Asking questions gives people time to *think* instead of *react*. It respectfully allows them to participate in a *conversation* instead of feeling attacked and responding defensively.

Asking questions is an art, however. "Not me" was, after all, a response to questions. Instead, I wish that I had been able to ask, "I see there's a mess here that needs to be cleaned up. Can I count on you to do that for me?" or "The trash needs to be taken out. Max, would you be willing to do that for me?"

- **Ask questions about the *behavior*.** ("Is that respectful behavior?" "Tell me how you see this working?")

Particularly in conflict and difficult conversations, we need to avoid labeling people based on how they behave. People are not their behavior and using behavior to label individuals is a good way to create defensiveness and divisiveness.

Instead of "He's a bully" it becomes "That bullying behavior…"

This is exceptionally useful within the Cage. When we label people as "racist," something that many people will deny, it is followed by adamant resistance and any constructive conversation comes to an end. Instead, we identify "racist behavior." This gives us an opening to the conversation instead of a stalling out. We certainly allow people to self-identify as racist but by changing our language we move toward respectful conversation that is necessary to have difficult conversations that create change (see Chapter 10).

- **Use "you" carefully and intentionally in questions or statements**. This is particularly true when we find ourselves in escalating situations or conflict. Speak in "I" statements. After all, it's the only perspective you can speak from.

Using "you" elicits the same response as pointing your finger at someone. It feels accusatory and is most often followed with further language of shame and blame. "I" statements allow us to speak from our perspective about our experience. This can create connection between people that allows the dialog to deepen.

Additionally, consider these:

- Use **observation language** ("I see you have not had a chance to take care of this report." "You seem upset/angry/happy/engaged, etc.")
- **Neutralize** descriptive language. This means we avoid "good/bad" or right/wrong" in our exploration of others' behavior or performance. In this way we avoid the tendency for individuals to need positive reinforcement from others about what they say and do. (In a situation where I am less than prepared, someone might respond by saying "I noticed when I asked you a question, you were silent. It would help me if you could think about these three things and get back to me.")

- **The story I make up about that is….** Starting with this we own our own perspective and recognize our natural tendency to make assumptions. We are also making room for others to help us change our story.
- **I'm curious about…**
- **Tell me more.**
- **That's not my experience…** instead of "you're wrong about…")
- **I'm wondering…**
- **Help me understand…**
- **Walk me through….** How that happened, how you see it, how we got here

Language is powerful. Another parenting story;

I had four kids (3 boys, 1 girl), blended family, so all aged within two years of each other. We lived out in the country, 40 minutes from their high school. There was one car. The general rule was that whoever put gas in it got to drive. The other three were passengers.

On this particular day, they were getting ready to come home. The daughter put gas in the car and consequently is sitting in the driver's seat. The oldest brother says, "I want to drive."

She says, "No, I put gas in it. I'm driving."

This goes back and forth for a few minutes before the oldest brother storms away.

Forty minutes later, they arrive home, minus a brother. I inquire and am told the story.

About 2 hours later, I still have heard nothing from the older brother. I start calling friends I know live near the school without any luck. It's a small town, so I now call the police station. "Oh yeah, we know where he hangs out. We'll drive by."

Fifteen minutes later I have a phone call, "What the f*** you call the cops for?"

I chose my words wisely, "I love you and you could be dead in a ditch somewhere. I was worried."

His response, "Oh."

This is the power of language.

Weaponized Language

Within the social justice and diversity field there are many words that have become weaponized. This means the words are used to blame, shame, gain advantage over, and otherwise "put people in their place." This is a reactive tendency that is the equivalent of name-calling.

Privilege is such a word. It has been used as an attack, like it's a bad thing.

Being born into a privilege experience does not make a person inherently good/bad, right/wrong, or... any more than being born into a target experience does.

It is about understanding your position within the Cage and making choices. When you know better, you do better. The more you know the more you can choose to do the things that help to blur the bars.

White fragility and snowflake are examples of words that have been used to parallel the negative connotation of privilege. They have become weapons thrown at one another in the same way that school children engage in name-calling.

This is not an effective use of language. It creates sides, you vs. me, us vs. them.

While it is true we will never all, thankfully, be of one mind (where's the diversity in that?) it is true we can learn and agree to be respectful to and with one another.

We've started that here in this text. Defining and explaining words and language is one of the first steps in establishing respectful communication. Regardless of the topic, whether we agree, accept, or like one another, we can be respectful.

It's about agreeing on what it means to be respectful and learning the behaviors that move us forward in that agreement.

That's what this new framework offers; a common experience with common language to explore and discuss, to disagree and dismantle, to find more ways and tools to move forward.

Myths & Misconceptions

There are a lot of myths and misconceptions that have taken hold in the diversity and social justice world over the last 60-80 years. We have touched on some of them in our journey so far but I want to take a hard look at them, why they aren't true and why they don't serve the movement of creating change.

Reverse Racism

There is no such thing as reverse racism (or reverse sexism, etc.). It's simply not possible. Remember that the -isms are the oppression. Based on our definition of oppression =

$$\text{prejudice} + \text{discrimination} + \text{systemic power}$$

target groups cannot oppress privilege groups. That's true as a system and it is true as an individual.

Let's take the example I get the most. A black professor grades white students more harshly than black and brown students. S/he does so openly even going so far as to say that white students start with 0% and have to earn their points while black and brown students start with 100% and have to lose their points.

This IS an example of prejudice. This IS an example of discrimination. But there is no systemic power. Sure, the professor has power in the classroom. But outside of the classroom, as a member of a target group, there is no systemic power.

It is still an example of poor teaching and wrong. But it is NOT racism.

This is true in the same way that bullying, by definition, requires the situation to have four things;

1. something mean done to another
2. something done with intention to harm
3. something done repeatedly

4. an imbalance of power in the relationship.

Without those four things, it isn't bullying. It is still wrong and in need of intervention but it isn't bullying.

Oppression works the same way.

Privilege = -ist

Someone who is a member of a privilege group is NOT automatically the – ist of the -ism. For example, all white people are not racists.

It bears repeating that, given the power of language, it is unhealthy and unwise to label people based on their behavior. Yes, white people have racist behaviors. That does not make them a racist. It makes them reactive to their internalizations of oppression and domination.

Black and brown people also have racist behaviors. That's also the result of internalized oppression and internalized domination.

This is the perpetuation of the system.

Consider the pull-down effect. **Also known as "crab bucket syndrome" this is often used to describe social situations where one person is trying to better themselves and others in the community attempt to pull them back down.**

This is a behavior that happens in our target groups. It is a direct result of internalized oppression and domination. It looks a lot like the -ist of the -ism.

Your membership in a privilege group does not automatically mean you are the -ist of the – ism. It does mean there is a lot of work to do to understand the power in your position in the Cage and how to use it.

When an assumption is made that "all white people are racist" it is hard to find a common path to make change that isn't driven from a position of guilt, blame, and shame. Guilt, shame, and blame are not the foundations of sustainable change, they stem from a wounded place.

They most often ultimately breed resentment and contempt if they are not effectively resolved.

Seeds planted in bad soil don't grow to healthy, productive plants.

Respectful communication that honors individuals across their intersectionality and values true diversity recognizes the need to come from an empowered place, not a wounded place. Coming from a wounded place only adds trauma to the trauma the Cage already inflicts. Trauma is not an effective tool for positive change.

Okay, now you're just making it palatable

Coming through a lens that respects all intersectional experiences as equal can seem like making difficult content palatable. Yet, if I invited you to dinner and served you really bad food what are the chances you would 1) eat it and 2) come back?

Progress isn't made through defensiveness, oppression olympics, shame and blame, or withdrawal. We have to find points of agreement to be willing to work together despite our differences in opinions, ideas, and ideals.

Simultaneously, without the gift of diversity – which is our differences in opinions, ideas, and ideals – we can't find the solution.

If we are sitting at a table talking about solutions and everyone agrees, someone is missing. That's the gift of diversity.

It doesn't mean we all agree or share the same vision or ideals. It means we make room for other ways of being.

Respectful behavior doesn't require me to like, accept, or even know you. It is the ground rules for common expectations in human interaction. Through the Cage it becomes easier to grasp what it means to be respectful to others who come from different experiences from my own.

I believe we can all agree on the ideals of respect and belonging, come to an understanding of what *we mean* by the words *respect* and *belonging*. We all want it for ourselves. It requires we understand others' want it too.

The Cage offers us a lens by which to peer into another's experience, to get a glimpse of something different. Being offered that glimpse requires respect and honor of those other experiences. That doesn't happen by misusing language or weaponizing words. It doesn't happen by holding desperately to my pain of oppression and historical trauma. It doesn't happen by causing others pain in the name of my right to be.

That's what this framework is all about; creating a framework that can be understood by all as a starting point from which we launch forward.

You wouldn't be the first to tell me this is palatable or idealist, or to insult my vision out of your own fear. But as long as you're talking to me, we are in relationship. That's the goal.

A Mono-Lens Approach

The most recent political movements have brought to light the pain and suffering of racism, particularly that inflicted upon Black Americans. The result has been a highly focused microscope on racism. Organizations and individuals see it as the crisis it is and, in response, have made it the central focus of their diversity efforts. This mono-lens approach is ineffective and potentially dangerous.

What happens when we focus on one -ism to the exclusion of all the others is we end up with the "what about me" syndrome. Other target groups rise up and potentially feel an increase in oppression. It can lead to divisiveness and a deafness of those who, in reality, could be great allies.

In my experience, there are a few explanations for this.

1. Part of the target group experience is a strong reality of being unheard. When another group becomes the hub of attention, the lack of being heard is emphasized, even exacerbated for

other target groups. The truth is that individuals and groups need to have their story heard to move forward. It is hard to let go of the suffering until we know our suffering has been recognized and honored (meaning it stops).

That isn't the experience of target groups within the Cage. Otherwise, they wouldn't be target groups anymore. So everyone raises their voice in an attempt to be heard. Within the din, none get heard.

2. This is another form of the pull-down effect as well. We can't have it, neither can you!
3. Additionally, as discussed early on, the Cage has to be fully dismantled. You can't just remove one -ism or portion of an -ism. It doesn't work like that. Historically, when a target group has a status change, there's not an elimination of the oppression. Consider the Irish who were targeted and oppressed when they first began immigrating to this country. Later, when they became more accepted as white, the oppression of others didn't stop. The Cage wasn't altered.

    This is the danger of the current mono-lens (Black Americans) within the mono-lens (Racism).

    For example, the focus on the black experience has done nothing for the continued oppression of Native Americans who continue to have to fight for their culture, language, and children.

4. Lastly, as I discussed previously, it's like a giant ball of knotted, twisted, yarn. If you pull on a single string, you actually tighten the entire system, increasing the number and tightness of knots. That's the effect of simply tugging on one -ism.

    Just as you have to go to the inside and pull the whole thing apart to deal with each of the strings collectively and individually, so we have to deal with the Cage. It isn't that we can't look first at race but to not look at the impact of class is a disservice to the systemic impact of racism. To not look at the intersectionality of the -isms (the full individual experience of the Cage) cuts off large parts of our experience.

This does NOT mean we can't focus on one -ism as the entry to the Cage. It can be argued that there is great benefit to understanding one -ism clearly and using it as a steppingstone to another. Yet to say there is one that needs to change first is a misperception. We arrive back at oppression olympics. Which means we are back at little to no progress.

Critical Race Theory

These three words, coined 40 years ago by Kimberlé Williams Crenshaw, have become a misunderstood battleground and sticking point. When you talk with people from both sides of the argument few can articulate what it is. There are very few environments where CRT is actually taught outside of college, mostly in the field of law.

Crenshaw defines it as "It is a way of seeing, attending to, accounting for, tracing and analyzing the ways that race is produced," she said, "the ways that racial inequality is facilitated, and the ways that our history has created these inequalities that now can be almost effortlessly reproduced unless we attend to the existence of these inequalities."

That means, Critical Race Theory (CRT) is, broadly, The Cage of Oppression through the lens of race. Specifically, it is the intersectionality of racism and classism and the systemic history of that intersect. It asks similar questions to this text; What do we do to make healthy change? Again, the difference is the mono-lens of race taken by CRT compared to the Cage which seeks to represent the system of oppression of which racism is a part.

In this way, the Cage broadens the conversation of CRT. In using a mono-lens effectively, CRT might then be bent slightly to look at the Cage collectively through class or ability or…. This would provide the opportunity to move through the Cage and truly understand the intersection of each of the tiers and bars. It might offer a clearer picture within, between, and across the bars.

The fear that has surfaced is the result of misunderstanding and lack of information. A theory is seldom something to fear, especially in education. It is a consideration, an exploration, and an attempt to explain something that is abstract. Sounds a lot like the Cage.

Those who oppose CRT claim it is the cause of divisiveness that makes white people (white wealthy men specifically) the bad guys. Their defensiveness becomes divisiveness.

Divisiveness is a thing that conversations (training, teaching, and learning) about diversity, equity, and inclusion can and do cause. My experience is that happens when the trainings are done poorly. It doesn't matter the content. It's about the delivery.

That means CRT isn't the problem, it's just taking the fall. As we begin to utilize the new framework of the Cage, we have the opportunity to introduce, expand, expound, and deepen our conversations so we, as a culture and society have a working understanding of all of these concepts, regardless of which side of the aisle we come from.

We just need more training

We have been doing diversity work since the 1940s. Considering we have been at it for over 70 years, we haven't made much progress.

If you don't believe me, search YouTube for "1940s anti-racist video" for an interesting contrast of then and now.

What's gone wrong?

After having served as "the cleanup crew" for diversity training gone awry, I have come to understand the reasons why it happens.

1. As discussed during the intro, part of the problem is that there has been a lot of pointing out what's wrong and demanding change without the teaching and learning of tools and skills.

2. Most "diversity training" hasn't followed the adult learning process which includes awareness, discord, awkward practice, integration, skilled practice, and mastery. It looks like this

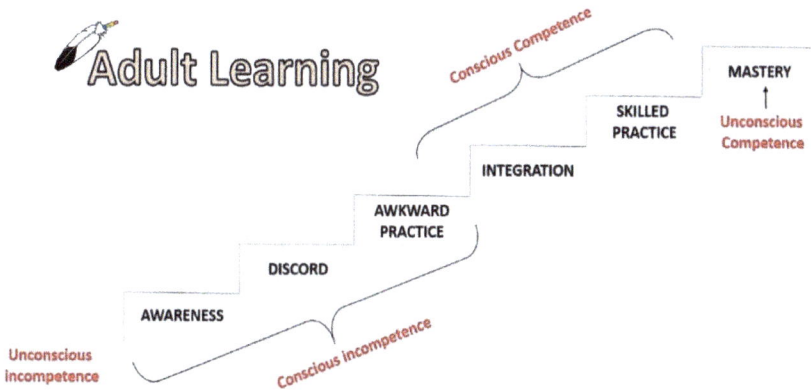

Notice this learning process starts with awareness and moves to discord. Discord is where I take what I am learning and try to fit it into what I already know. We talked about this when we looked at resistance.

Notice that after discord comes awkward practice. That implies there is something to practice, ergo, we must be learning tools and skills to be able to practice something. And *practice* is the key to integration.

Notice the competency levels in red. Prior to awareness, there is unconscious incompetence (I don't know what I don't know). All the way through awkward practice is conscious incompetence (I know I don't know it). Only through awkward practice do we, not only move into integration, but that's how we get to conscious competence (I know it and can do it).

The reality is most diversity training doesn't move the process through to integration. People don't get to practice, even if they're offered tools. Without that, folks walk out of training with the "wow that was great" feeling but when they get back to life, they don't know how to apply it.

Additionally, when people are left in discord after being made aware of things that cause them to feel guilt, shame, blame, and judgement, they generally become discontent. It leads to everything from disengagement and withdrawal to violence.

3. Content is taught through a shame and blame model that causes, not just the discomfort of moving through painful and difficult stuff, but also the hijacking of the amygdala which means no learning is going to happen. This can actually be a traumatic experience for people from both target and privilege.
4. Trying to teach inclusion through an exclusionary model. When we stand up to say, "Everyone must think this way" we are creating parameters of exclusion. If you don't think like this, you aren't doing it right. Diversity, by definition, has to allow for multiple perspectives to be seen and honored. We don't have to agree with, like, or accept all of the perspectives. We, of course, require boundaries that keep everyone psychologically and physically safe. But there is room for disagreement. There is a way for us all to cohabitate.

It's best if I stay quiet

This is one of the consequences of diversity experiences that have not gone well. In response to the shame and blame model, people from privilege groups become afraid of "getting it wrong." They already feel beat up and they don't want to expose themselves to anymore. They decide that it is best to say nothing and do nothing.

Sometimes it's a response to being "called out." I have never seen this done without shame and blame. It identifies the individual as having done something inappropriate and harmful. Instead of making it a teaching moment, it simply becomes an excuse to publicly humiliate them. Anyone subjected to that type of behavior is most likely to shrink back and make no more attempts at interrupting the Cage.

When we remember that people are not their behavior, it becomes clear that a more respectful approach is to call the behavior forward. In this way, the mistake is pointed out and the healthier alternative is brought into the conversation. In this life-long process of dismantling the Cage, it has to be safe to make mistakes. When it isn't, people stop trying – trying to learn, trying to interrupt, trying to get it right. When people stop trying, we are guaranteed oppression will continue.

One and Done: check the box

Organizations often go looking for trainers to come in and do the diversity training. You know what I mean. It's the once a year, or every couple years, event that is part of the strategic plan and a weak attempt to align diversity goals with organizational activities. This is what I call "drive-by training."

If you think that having anyone come in for a few hours once in a while will make any change in your organization than you might consider researching effective change. That's not how it's done.

Remember the Adult Learning Process we outlined earlier? I have studied and developed programs that support what it takes to teach people skills and tools that they will use effectively. You can teach one tool, to the point of awkward practice, maybe entering integration, in 90 minutes. That's in a group with a ratio of no higher than 30 learners to 1 teacher.

The tools for successful change in social justice are innumerable. Different roles and different people will need different tools. It's not a one and done. There's no simple way to check the box if you truly want to do the work of moving an organization into a culture of equity and respect.

The work I do teachers people the skills of respect and belonging. This shifts an organizational culture to one of equity and respect. How? The outcomes of a workplace that creates a sense of belonging for everyone and is respectful are justice and dignity. These are the desired outcomes of diversity and social justice work.

Teaching tools of respect and belonging, allowing people to practice, to make mistakes, to learn from one another, and to arrive at a destination of common experience, common language is a prolonged process that requires a commitment of time and resources.

One and done doesn't work. Checking the box isn't the point. The sooner we all accept that reality and plan for what is needed, the quicker change will take hold at the systemic level.

Tools of Change

The Cage of Oppression is a framework by which we can create meaningful change in social justice. It provides the foundational common experience. I've used these words before but what exactly do I mean by them?

When we come together to learn, we come from a myriad of experiences, perspectives, learnings, and history. We could clearly identify those differences as part of our diversity and much of that "myriad" stems from our intersectional experience within the Cage. AND most of us don't even know how much of our experience really is influenced and driven by the Cage, particularly if we have never been taught about it.

By teaching and using the Cage of Oppression as the framework, it becomes our common experience. The language and vocabulary, once integrated, becomes our common language. This is a solid beginning for big moves forward. It's as if we are all standing on the same hill looking in the same direction. While some will notice things differently, we have a common starting point. As we move forward, we are moving in the same direction and can talk about what we see, feel, think, and experience. We can create change and we can entertain possibilities we didn't even know existed. It can be pretty amazing, particularly when we don't agree!

Within this framework is the core concept of respect. There is no hierarchy of oppression and no consequential need for olympics. It begins with seeing the systemic perspective and then focusing into the individual experience of intersectionality. It is respecting that every experience within the Cage is valid, that each voice needs to be heard as part of the solution, and that moving forward is a collective affair.

By coming through the lenses of respect and belonging, we begin with a focus on behavior. We don't challenge beliefs or identities. We ground ourselves in learning tools of clear communication and effective and fair management of conflict. We understand ourselves first, learning how to recognize our own fears, beliefs, and motivations. We explore ways in which we can empower and enlighten ourselves and each other.

This gentler introduction allows for deeper conversation later. It is in these later conversations we can begin to challenge beliefs, our own as well as those of others. We find our strengths and passions and stand in the power of what we have learned together. From here, the work grows. Others add to what they've been taught, the Cage becomes a malleable tool that grows and deepens with the experience and understanding that time, effort, and commitment bring.

How long does it take to get to those deep conversations? In my experience it generally takes a committed group of people between two and a half and three years to get to the deeper conversations of committed change. In the big picture, that's not long. If we move there together, it might be possible to move some mountains in my lifetime.

That's what this work is for, what this text is designed to do; to provide foundations that serve as the leaping point for more.

This book is written for people of all perspectives to read. Not because we have to agree, but because we need a common experience and common language with which to have meaningful conversation, to engage in disagreement in a way that does more than just drive wedges between us. Won't it be so interesting and exciting when our disagreements lead to sustainable change instead of more arguments and misunderstandings? That's where we can go with this common experience, common language, and a leaping off point.

The next several months I will be following up this book with an eBook series, Deep Dive, where I intend to begin that next journey of deepening the conversation. Some of the topics intended have been introduced here. Some will be new. If you have your own questions, suggestions, wishes to know how I might use the lens of the Cage to describe something, please let me know. This is, after all, our journey together.

Thank you for your time and attention. The Appendix that follows is material noted in the text, included to support your full understanding.

I look forward to your thoughts, reviews, and comments. Write them on Amazon, send me an email, connect with me on LinkedIn or Facebook. I always love respectful conversation, especially if it involves a challenge, push back, or a fun question.

Here's to learning and practicing the tools of respect and belonging so we can create justice and dignity for all.

Appendix

OPRESSION   *by Marilyn Frye*

It is a fundamental claim of feminism that women are oppressed. The word "oppression" is a strong word. It repels and attracts. It is dangerous and dangerously fashionable and endangered. It is much misused, and sometimes not innocently.

The statement that women are oppressed is frequently met with the claim that men are oppressed too. We hear that oppressing is oppressive to those who oppress as well as those they oppress. Some men cite as evidence of their oppression their much-advertised inability to cry. It is tough, we are told, to be masculine. When the stresses and frustrations of being a man are cited as evidence that oppressors are oppressed by their oppressing, the word "oppression" is being stretched to meaninglessness; it is treated as though its scope includes any and all human experience of limitation or suffering, no matter the cause, degree or consequence. Once such usage has been put over on us, then if ever we deny that any person or group is oppressed, we seem to imply that we think they never suffer and have no feelings. We are accused of insensitivity; even of bigotry. For women, such accusation is particularly intimidating, since sensitivity is one of the few virtues that has been assigned to us. If we are found insensitive, we may fear we have no redeeming traits at all and perhaps are not real women. Thus are we silenced before we begin: the name of our situation drained of meaning and our guilt mechanisms tripped.

But this is nonsense. Human beings can be miserable without being oppressed, and it is perfectly consistent to deny that a person or group is oppressed without denying that they have feelings or that they suffer.

We need to think clearly about this oppression, and there is much that mitigates against this. I do not want to undertake to prove that women are oppressed (or that men are not), but I want to make clear what is being said when we say it. We need this word, this concept, and we need it to be sharp and sure.

I

The root of the word "oppression" is the element "press." *The press of the crowd; pressed into military service; to press a pair of pants; printing press; press the button.*Presses are used to mold things or flatten them or reduce them in bulk, sometimes to reduce them by squeezing out the gases or liquids in them. Something pressed is something caught between or among forces and barriers which are so related to each other that jointly they restrain, restrict or prevent the thing's motion or mobility. Mold. Immobilize. Reduce.

The mundane experience of the oppressed provides another clue. One of the most characteristic and ubiquitous features of the world as experienced by oppressed people is the double bind — situations in which options are reduced to a very few and all of them expose one to penalty, censure or deprivation. For example, it is often a requirement upon oppressed people that we smile and be cheerful. If we comply, we signal our docility and our acquiescence in our situation. We need not, then, be taken note of. We acquiesce in being made invisible, in our occupying no space. We participate in our own erasure. On the other hand, anything but the sunniest countenance exposes us to being perceived as mean, bitter, angry or dangerous. This means, at the least, that we may be found "difficult" or unpleasant to work with, which is enough to cost one one's livelihood; at worst, being seen as mean, bitter, angry or dangerous has been known to result in rape, arrest, beating, and murder. One can only choose to risk one's preferred form and rate of annihilation.

Another example: It is common in the United States that women, especially younger women, are in a bind where neither sexual activity nor sexual inactivity is all right. If she is heterosexually active, a woman is open to censure and punishment for being loose, unprincipled or a whore. The "punishment" comes in the form of criticism, snide and embarrassing remarks, being treated as an easy lay by men, scorn from her more restrained female friends. She may have to lie to hide her behavior from her parents. She must juggle the risks of unwanted pregnancy and dangerous contraceptives. On the other hand, if she refrains from heterosexual activity, she is fairly constantly harassed by men who try to persuade her into it and pressure her into it and pressure her to "relax" and "let her hair down"; she is threatened with labels like "frigid," "uptight," "man-hater," "bitch," and "cocktease." The same parents who would be disapproving of her sexual activity may be worried by her inactivity because it suggests she is not or will not be popular, or is not sexually normal. She may be charged with lesbianism. If a woman is raped, then if she has been heterosexually active she is subject to the presumption that she liked it (since her activity is presumed to show that she likes sex), and if she has not been heterosexually active, she is subject to the presumption that she liked it (since she is supposedly "repressed and frustrated"). Both heterosexual activity and heterosexual nonactivity are likely to be taken as proof that you wanted to be raped, and hence, of course, weren't *really* raped at all. You can't win. You are caught in a bind, caught between systematically related pressures.

Women are caught like this, too, by networks of forces and barriers that expose one to penalty, loss or contempt whether one works outside the home or not, is on welfare or not, bears children or not, raises children or not, marries or not, stays married or not, is heterosexual, lesbian, both or neither. Economic necessity; confinement to racial and/or sexual job ghettos; sexual harassment; sex discrimination; pressures of competing expectations and judgements about *women*, *wives* and *mothers* (in the society at large, in racial and ethnic subcultures and in one's own mind); dependence (full or partial) on husbands, parents or the state; commitment to political ideas; loyalties to racial or ethnic or other "minority" groups; the demands of the self-respect and responsibilities to others. Each of these factors exists in complex tension with every other, penalizing or prohibiting all of the apparently available options. And nipping at one's heels, always, is the endless pack of little things. If one dresses one way, one is subject to the assumption that one is advertising one's sexual availability; if one dresses another way, one appears to "not care about oneself" or to be "unfeminine." If one uses "strong language," one invites categorization as a "lady" – one too delicately constituted to cope with robust speech or the realities to which it presumably refers.

The experience of oppressed people is that the living of one's life is confined and shaped by forces and barriers which are not accidental or occasional and hence avoidable, but are systematically related to each other in such a way as to catch one between and among them and restrict or penalize motion in any direction. It is the experience of being caged in: all avenues, in every direction, are blocked or booby trapped.

Cages. Consider a birdcage. If you look very closely at just one wire in the cage, you cannot see the other wires. If your conception of what is before you is determined by this myopic focus, you could look at that one wire, up and down the length of it, and be unable to see why a bird would not just fly around the wire any time it wanted to go somewhere. Furthermore, even if, one day at a time, you myopically inspected each wire, you still could not see why a bird would gave trouble going past the wires to get anywhere. There is no physical property of any one wire, *nothing* that the closest scrutiny could discover, that will reveal how a bird could be inhibited or harmed by it except in the most accidental way. It is only when you step back, stop looking at the wires one by one, microscopically, and take a macroscopic view of the whole cage, that you can see why the bird does not go anywhere; and then you will see it in a moment. It will require no great subtlety of mental powers. It is perfectly obvious that the bird is surrounded by a network of systematically related barriers, no one of which would be the least hindrance to its flight, but which, by their relations to each other, are as confining as the solid walls of a dungeon.

It is now possible to grasp one of the reasons why oppression can be hard to see and recognize: one can study the elements of an oppressive structure with great care and some good will without seeing the structure as a whole, and hence without seeing or being able to understand that one is looking at a cage and that there are people there who are caged, whose motion and mobility are restricted, whose lives are shaped and reduced.

The arresting of vision at a microscopic level yields such common confusion as that about the male door-opening ritual. This ritual, which is remarkably widespread across classes and races, puzzles many people, some of whom do and some of whom do not find it offensive. Look at the scene of the two people approaching a door. The male steps slightly ahead and opens the door. The male holds the door open while the female glides through. Then the male goes through. The door closes after them. "Now how," one innocently asks, "can those crazy womens libbers say that is oppressive? The guy *removed* a barrier to the lady's smooth and unruffled progress." But each repetition of this ritual has a place in a pattern, in fact in several patterns. One has to shift the level of one's perception in order to see the whole picture.

The door-opening pretends to be a helpful service, but the helpfulness is false. This can be seen by noting that it will be done whether or not it makes any practical sense. Infirm men and men burdened with packages will open doors for able-bodied women who are free of physical burdens. Men will impose themselves awkwardly and jostle everyone in order to get to the door first. The act is not determined by convenience or grace. Furthermore, these very numerous acts of unneeded or even noisome "help" occur in counterpoint to a pattern of men not being helpful in many practical ways in which women might welcome help. What *women* experience is a world in which gallant princes charming commonly make a fuss about being helpful and providing small services when help and services are of little or no use, but in which there are rarely ingenious and adroit princes at hand when substantial assistance is really wanted either in mundane affairs or in situations of threat, assault or terror. There is no help with the (his) laundry; no help typing a report at 4:00 a.m.; no help in mediating disputes among relatives or children. There is nothing but advice that women should stay indoors after dark, be chaperoned by a man, or when it comes down to it, "lie back and enjoy it."

The gallant gestures have no practical meaning. Their meaning is symbolic. The door-opening and similar services provided are services which really are needed by people who are for one reason or another incapacitated – unwell, burdened with parcels, etc. So the message is that women are incapable. The detachment of the acts from the concrete realities of what women need and do not need is a vehicle for the message that women's actual needs and interests are unimportant or irrelevant. Finally, these gestures imitate the behavior of servants toward masters and thus mock women, who are in most respects the servants and caretakers of men. The message of the false helpfulness of male gallantry is female dependence, the invisibility or insignificance of women, and contempt for women.

One cannot see the meanings of these rituals if one's focus is riveted upon the individual event in all its particularity, including the particularity of the individual man's present conscious intentions and motives and the individual woman's conscious perception of the event in the moment. It seems sometimes that people take a deliberately myopic view and fill their eyes with things seen microscopically in order not to see macroscopically. At any rate, whether it is deliberate or not, people can and do fail to see the oppression of women because they fail to see macroscopically and hence fail to see the various elements of the situation as systematically related in larger schemes.

As the cageness of the birdcage is a macroscopic phenomenon, the oppressiveness of the situations in which women live our various and different lives is a macroscopic phenomenon. Neither can be *seen* from a microscopic perspective. But when you look macroscopically you can see it – a network of forces and barriers which are systematically related and which conspire to the immobilization, reduction and molding of women and the lives we live.

II

The image of the cage helps convey one aspect of the systematic nature of oppression. Another is the selection of occupants of the cages, and analysis of this aspect also helps account for the invisibility of the oppression of women.

It is as a woman (or as a Chicana/o or as a Black or Asian or lesbian) that one is entrapped.

"Why can't I go to the park; you let Jimmy go!"

"Because it's not safe for girls."

"I want to be a secretary, not a seamstress; I don't want to learn to make dresses."

"There's no work for negroes in that line; learn a skill where you can earn your living."!

When you question why you are being blocked, why this barrier is in your path, the answer has not to do with individual talent or merit, handicap or failure; it has to do with your membership in some category understood as a "natural" or "physical" category. The "inhabitant" of the "cage" is not an individual but a group, all those of a certain category. If an individual is oppressed, it is in virtue of being a member of a group or category of people that is systematically reduced, molded, immobilized. Thus, to recognize a person as oppressed, one has to see that individual *as* belonging to a group of a certain sort.

There are many things which can encourage or inhibit perception of someone's membership in the sort of group or category in question here. In particular, it seems reasonable to suppose that if one of the devices of restriction and definition of the group is that of physical confinement or segregation, the confinement and separation would encourage recognition of the group as a group. This in turn would encourage the macroscopic focus which enables one to recognize oppression and encourages the individuals' identification and solidarity with other individuals of the group or category. But physical confinement and segregation of the group as a group is not common to all oppressive structures, and when an oppressed group is geographically and demographically dispersed the perception of it as a group is inhibited. There may be little or no thing in the situations of the individuals encouraging the macroscopic focus which would reveal the unity of the structure bearing down on all members of that group. *

(*Coerced assimilation is in fact one of the *policies* available to an oppressing group in its effort to reduce and/or annihilate another group. This tactic is used by the U.S. government, for instance, on the American Indians.)

A great many people, female and male and of every race and class, simply do not believe that *woman* is a category of oppressed people, and I think that this is in part because they have been fooled by the dispersal and assimilation of women throughout and into the systems of class and race which organize men. Our simply being dispersed makes it difficult for women to have knowledge of each other and hence difficult to recognize the shape of our common cage. The dispersal and assimilation of women throughout economic classes and races also divides us against each other practically and economically and thus attaches *interest* to the inability to see: for some, jealousy of their benefits, and for some, resentment of the others' advantages.

To get past this, it helps to notice that in fact women of all races and classes *are* together in a ghetto of sorts. There is a women's place, a sector, which is inhabited by women of all classes and races, and it is not defined by geographical boundaries but by function. The function is the service of men and men's interests as men define them, which includes the bearing and rearing of children. The details of the service and the working conditions vary by race and class, for men of different races and classes have different interests, perceive their interests differently, and express their needs and demands in different rhetorics, dialects and languages. But there are also some constants.

Whether in lower, middle or upper-class home or work situations, women's service work always includes personal service (the work of maids, butlers, cooks, personal secretaries),* sexual service (including provision for his genital sexual needs and bearing his children, but also including "being nice," "being attractive for him," etc.), and ego service (encouragement, support, praise, attention). Women's service work also is characterized everywhere by the fatal combination of responsibility and powerlessness: we are held responsible and we hold ourselves responsible for good outcomes for men and children in almost every respect though we have in almost no case power adequate to that project. The details of the subjective experience of this servitude are local. They vary with economic class and race and ethnic tradition as well as the personalities of the men in question. So also are the details of the forces which coerce our tolerance of this servitude particular to the different situations in which different women live and work.

(* At higher class levels women may not *do* all these kinds of work, but are generally still responsible for hiring and supervising those who do it These services are still, in these cases, women's responsibility.)

All this is not to say that women do not have, assert and manage sometimes to satisfy our own interests, nor to deny that in some cases and in some respects women's independent interests do overlap with men's. But at every race/class level and even across race/class lines men do not serve women as women serve men. "Women's sphere" maybe understood as the "service sector," taking the latter expression much more widely and deeply than is usual in discussions of the economy.

III

It seems to be the human condition that in one degree or another we all suffer frustration and limitation, all encounter unwelcome barriers, and all are damaged and hurt in various ways. Since we are a social species, almost all of our behavior and activities are structured by more than individual inclination and the conditions of the planet and its atmosphere. No human is free of social structures, nor (perhaps) would happiness consist in such freedom. Structure consists of boundaries, limits and barriers; in a structured whole, some motions and changes are possible, and others are not. If one is looking for an excuse to dilute the word 'oppression', one can use the fact of social structure as an excuse and say that everyone is oppressed. But if one would rather get clear about what oppression is and is not, one needs to sort out the sufferings, harms and limitations and figure out which are elements of oppression and which are not.

From what I have already said here, it is clear that if one wants to determine whether a particular suffering, harm or limitation is part of someone's being oppressed, one has to look at it *in context* in order to tell whether it is an element in an oppressive structure: one has to see if it is part of an enclosing structure of forces and barriers which tends to the immobilization and reduction of a group or category of people. One has to look at how the barrier or force fits with others and to whose benefit or detriment it works. As soon as one looks at examples, it becomes obvious that not everything which frustrates or limits a person is oppressive, and not every harm or damage is due to or contributes to oppression.

If a rich white playboy who lives off income from his investments in South African diamond mines should break a leg in a skiing accident at Aspen and wait in pain in a blizzard for hours before he is rescued, we may assume that in that period he suffers. But the suffering comes to an end; his leg is repaired by the best surgeon money can buy and he is soon recuperating in a lavish suite, sipping Chivas Regal. Nothing in this picture suggests a structure of barriers and forces. He is a member of several oppressor groups and does not suddenly become oppressed because he is injured and in pain. Even if the accident was caused by someone's malicious negligence, and hence someone can be blamed for it and morally faulted, that person still has not been an agent of oppression.

Consider also the restriction of having to drive one's vehicle on a certain side of the road. There is no doubt that this restriction is almost unbearably frustrating at times, when one's lane is not moving and the other lane is clear. There are surely times, even, when abiding by this regulation would have harmful consequences. But the restriction is obviously wholesome for most of us most of the time. The restraint is imposed for our benefit, and does benefit us; its operation tends to encourage our *continued* motion, not to immobilize us. The limits imposed by traffic regulations are limits most of us would cheerfully impose on ourselves given that we knew others would follow them too. They are part of a structure which shapes our behavior, not to our reduction and immobilization, but rather to the protection of our continued ability to move and act as we will.

Another example: The boundaries of a racial ghetto in an American city serve to some extent to keep white people from going in, as well as to keep ghetto dwellers from going out. A particular white citizen may be frustrated or feel deprived because s/he cannot stroll around there and enjoy the "exotic" aura of a "foreign" culture, or shop for bargains in the ghetto swap shops. In fact, the existence of the ghetto, of racial segregation, does deprive the white person of knowledge and harm her/his character by nurturing unwarranted feelings of superiority. But this does not make the white person in this situation a member of an oppressed race or a person oppressed because of her/his race. One must look at the barrier. It limits the activities and the access of those on both sides of it (though to different degrees). But it is a product of the intention, planning and action of whites for the benefit of whites, to secure and maintain privileges that are available to whites generally, as members of the dominant and privileged group. Though the existence of the barrier has some bad consequences for whites, the barrier does not exist in systematic relationship with other barriers and forces forming a structure oppressive to whites; quite the contrary. It is part of a structure which oppresses the ghetto dwellers and thereby (and by white intention) protects and furthers white interests as dominant white culture understands them. This barrier is not oppressive to whites, even though it is a barrier to whites.

Barriers have different meanings to those on opposite sides of them, even though they are barriers to both. The physical walls of a prison no more dissolve to let an outsider in than to let an insider out, but for the insider they are confining and limiting while to the outsider they may mean protection from what s/he takes to be threats posed by insiders-

freedom from harm or anxiety. A set of social and economic barriers and forces separating two groups may be felt, even painfully, by members of both groups and yet may mean confinement to one and liberty and enlargement of opportunity to the other.

The service sector of the wives/mommas/assistants/girls is almost exclusively a woman-only sector; its boundaries not only enclose women but to a very great extent keep men out. Some men sometimes encounter this barrier and experience it as a restriction on their movements, their activities, their control or their choices of "lifestyle." Thinking they might like the simple nurturant life (which they may imagine to be quite free of stress, alienation and hard work), and feeling deprived since it seems closed to them, they thereupon announce the discovery that they are oppressed, too, by "sex roles." But that barrier is erected and maintained by men, for the benefit of men. It consists of cultural and economic forces and pressures in a culture and economy controlled by men in which, at every economic level and in all racial and ethnic subcultures, economy, tradition-and even ideologies of liberation-work to keep at least local culture and economy in male control.*

(* Of course this is complicated by race and class. Machismo and "Black manhood" politics seem to help keep Latin or Black men in control of more cash than Latin or Black women control; but these politics seem to me also to ultimately help keep the larger economy in *white* male control.)

The boundary that sets apart women's sphere is maintained and promoted by men generally for the benefit of men generally, and men generally do benefit from its existence, even the man who bumps into it and complains of the inconvenience. That barrier is protecting his classification and status as a male, as superior, as having a right to sexual access to a female or females. It protects a kind of citizenship which is superior to that of females of his class and race, his access to a wider range of better paying and higher status work, and his right to prefer unemployment to the degradation of doing lower status or "women's" work.

If a person's life or activity is affected by some force or barrier that person encounters, one may not conclude that the person is oppressed simply because the person encounters that barrier or force; nor simply because the encounter is unpleasant, frustrating or painful to that person at that time; nor simply because the existence of the barrier or force, or the processes which maintain or apply it, serve to deprive that person of something of value. One must look at the barrier or force and answer certain questions about it. Who constructs and maintains it? Whose interests are served by its existence? Is it part of a structure which tends to confine, reduce and immobilize some group? Is the individual a member of the confined group? Various forces, barriers and limitations a person may encounter or live with may be part of an oppressive structure or not, and if they are, that person may be on either the oppressed or the oppressor side of it. One cannot tell which by how loudly or how little the person complains.

IV

Many of the restrictions and limitations we live with are more or less internalized and self-monitored, and are part of our adaptations to the requirements and expectations imposed by the needs and tastes and tyrannies of others. I have in mind such things as women's cramped postures and attenuated strides and men's restraint of emotional self-expression (except for anger). Who gets what out of the practice of those disciplines, and who imposes what penalties for improper relaxations of them? What are the rewards of this self-discipline?

Can men cry? Yes, in the company of women. If a man cannot cry, it is in the company of men that he cannot cry. It is men, not women, who require this restraint; and men not only require it, they reward it. The man who maintains a steely or tough or laid-back demeanor (all are forms which suggest invulnerability) marks himself as a member of the male community and is esteemed by other men. Consequently, the maintenance of that demeanor contributes to the man's self-esteem. It is felt as good, and he can feel good about himself. The way this restriction fits into the structures of men's lives is as one of the socially required behaviors which, if carried off, contribute to their acceptance and respect by significant others and to their own self-esteem. It is to their benefit to practice this discipline.

Consider, by comparison, the discipline of women's cramped physical postures and attenuated stride. This discipline can be relaxed in the company of women; it generally is at its most strenuous in the company of men. * Like men's emotional restraint, women's physical restraint is required by men. But unlike the case of men's emotional restraint, women's physical restraint is not rewarded. What do we get for it? Respect and esteem and acceptance? No. They mock us and parody our mincing steps. We look silly, incompetent, weak and generally contemptible. Our exercise of this discipline tends to low esteem and low self-esteem. It does not benefit us. It fits in a network of behaviors through which we constantly announce to others our membership in a lower caste and our unwillingness and/or inability to defend our bodily or moral integrity. It is degrading and part of a pattern of degradation.

Acceptable behavior for both groups, men and women, involves a required restraint that seems in itself silly and perhaps damaging. But the social effect is drastically different. The woman's restraint is part of a structure oppressive to women; the man's restraint is part of a structure oppressive to women.

(*Cf., *Let's Take Back OUT Space: "Female" and "Male " Body Language as a Result of Patriarchal Structures,* by Marianne Wex (Frauenliteratureverlag Hermine Fees, West Germany, 1979), especially p. 173. This remarkable book presents literally thousands of candid photographs of women and men, in public, seated, standing and lying down. It vividly demonstrates the very systematic differences in women's and men's postures and gestures.)

V

One is marked for application of oppressive pressures by one's membership in some group or category. Much of one's suffering and frustration befalls one partly or largely because one is a member of that category. In the case at hand, it is the category, *woman.* Being a woman is a major factor in my not having a better job than I do; being a woman selects me as a likely victim of sexual assault or harassment; it is my being a woman that reduces the power of my anger to a proof of my insanity. If a woman has little or no economic or political power, or achieves little of what she wants to achieve a major causal factor in this is that she is a woman. For any woman of any race or economic class, being a woman is significantly attached to whatever disadvantages and deprivations she suffers, be they great or small.

None of this is the case with respect to a person's being a man. Simply being a man is not what stands between him and a better job; whatever assaults and harassments he is subject to, being male is not what selects him for victimization; being male is not a factor which would make his anger impotent-quite the opposite. If a man has little or no material or political power, or achieves little of what he wants to achieve, his being male is no part of the explanation. Being male is something he has going/or him, even if race or class or age or disability is going against him.

Women are oppressed, as *women.* Members of certain racial and/or economic groups and classes, both the males and the females, are oppressed as members of those races and/or classes. But men are not oppressed *as men*.

... and isn't it strange that any of us should have been confused and mystified about such a simple thing?

NOTES

1. This example is derived from *Daddy Was A Number Runner,* by Louise Meriwether (Prentice-Hall, Englewood Cliffs, New Jersey, 1970), p.144.

From: Marilyn Frye, *The Politics of Reality* (Trumansburg, N.Y.,: The Crossing Press, 1983).

Goff article on childhood innocence

https://www.apa.org/pubs/journals/releases/psp-a0035663.pdf

Between the Bars

ABOUT THE AUTHOR

Leah R. Kyaio, M.Ed is CEO/Founder of With Respect LLC is the architect of Diversity Done Differently and Teach/Lead Like Their Lives Depend On It. She has been a teacher and trainer for more than twenty-five years. Leah operates from a perspective of tools-driven learning as the way to drive real change. As a result, everything she does is about building, nurturing, and expanding your personal and professional toolbox. Additionally, Leah leans into the research and brings it all together in new and exciting ways that serve to make learning clear, fun, and life changing. Her work comes through a lens of resilience, integrating the science of trauma and recovery. Best of all, she uses everything she teaches in her everyday life, practicing what she teaches. Leah also believes in the symbiotic relationship of learning which means we are all simultaneously teachers and learners. She loves nothing more than to engage in dialog that explores what you think and how you see your learning. Be sure to take any opportunity you can to enjoy Leah's writing, teaching, training, and – especially – laughing.

Through her business, With Respect LLC, she provides speaking, professional development training, consulting, and executive coaching. You can find her on Facebook, LinkedIn, and at https://with-respect.com.

www.ingramcontent.com/pod-product-compliance
Lightning Source LLC
Chambersburg PA
CBHW070351270326
41926CB00017B/4090